Ethnic Matching

Ethnic Matching

Academic Success of Students of Color

Donald Easton-Brooks

ROWMAN & LITTLEFIELD
Lanham • Boulder • New York • London

Published by Rowman & Littlefield
An imprint of The Rowman & Littlefield Publishing Group, Inc.
4501 Forbes Boulevard, Suite 200, Lanham, Maryland 20706
www.rowman.com

6 Tinworth Street, London SE11 5AL, United Kingdom

Copyright © 2019 by Donald Easton-Brooks

British Library Cataloguing in Publication Information Available

Library of Congress Cataloging-in-Publication Data Available
ISBN: 978-1-4758-3965-4 (cloth : alk. paper)
ISBN: 978-1-4758-3966-1 (paper : alk. paper)
ISBN: 978-1-4758-3967-8 (electronic)

♾™ The paper used in this publication meets the minimum requirements of American National Standard for Information Sciences—Permanence of Paper for Printed Library Materials, ANSI/NISO Z39.48–1992.

Printed in the United States of America

To my three sons (Dawson, Devyn, and Daniel) who understand the purpose of the work that I do and are willing to sacrifice their time with me so I can write this book because they also understand the value of using our privilege and knowledge to assist others. Our saying is that "God will judge us by what we do with our privilege." To my wife, Lori, my comfort and mother of these wonderful boys; without Lori, the attitudes, patience, and understanding of my three sons would not be remotely possible. Her strength, encouragement, and commitment to justice and human rights help to make my work possible.

Contents

Foreword

"Ethnic Matching": Intriguing Idea, Challenging Practice

At first look, Donald Easton-Brooks's proposal of "ethnic matching" for improving the "academic success of students of color" in US public schools appears to be rather easy to promote or to oppose. However, closer scrutiny reveals a recommendation of depth and complexity, of invitation and challenge, of innovation and convention.

Some of his recommendations are reminiscent of common occurrences within the legacies of Black educators teaching Black students in pre-desegregation eras (for example, Foster, 1997; Siddle Walker, 1996); of recent analyses of ethnic, racial, and cultural resilience and regeneration offered by scholars from different groups of color; and of programs of study emphasizing personal deportment, political and cultural consciousness, socioemotional wellness, and academic performance of students in ethnic heritage colleges and universities, such as those serving primarily Blacks and Native Americans (for example, Ashley, Williams, & Ingrum, 2009; Fleming, 1991; McCarty & Lee, 2014).

Some educators are likely to react negatively to the idea of ethnic matching, which may appear to them as endorsing educational segregation based on race. Others may react smugly with assumed validation of their attitude, saying, "I told you so. Whites can't teach students of color." European American (White) teachers who experience anxieties and feelings of not belonging with regard to teaching students of color may feel vindicated and exempted from any related obligations. These reactions operate on the fallacious assumption that race and ethnicity are synonymous and that teachers' shared racial identity with their students will ensure pedagogical effectiveness and academic success. Shared racial identity is important in educating students of color, but it is not sufficient.

Teachers of color and others who understand the interactive complexities of color, culture, and education are needed for better educating students of color. They are pivotal in breaking down fears and misconceptions about interracial relations generally and within educational contexts specifically. This is the more profound message presented in this book—that cultural congruency between home and school improves the school achievement of students of color. Teachers and other users need to read this book carefully and deeply to avoid unfounded and superficial assumptions about race, ethnicity, and culture in teaching and learning.

Evidence derived from personal narratives, empirical data, and experiential memories (such as that presented by Easton-Brooks and other scholars too) show that studying under the tutelage of culturally responsive teachers generates multiple kinds of positive achievements for students of color. These are the central focus of this book. As such, Easton-Brooks explicates what teachers of color (and others too) do pedagogically and the ways they relate with students of color that make the difference between academic success and failure.

The essence of these pedagogical and relational behaviors is ethnic matching, or culturally responsive teaching. Stated differently, this success is nested in cohesion between home and school cultures in both teaching and learning. As Jaime Escalante said about his teaching poor urban Latinx, it involves helping students to simultaneously develop cultural and experiential roots and wings and habitually includes mirrors of the self and windows to others (see Dembski & Thomas, 2016; Mathews, 1989). Who is better equipped to do this than teachers who know, respect, and use the cultural heritages, ethnic identities, and experiential backgrounds of their racially and socially diverse students in academic teaching and learning!

While compelling evidence of the positive effects of Blacks teaching Black students specifically, and teachers of color working with students of color generally, are presented throughout this book, some questions and challenges also are implied. Who else can and should be ethnically matched for the sake of improved academic success? Are there historical precedents for this process and, if so, what can be learned from them for current and future use? Can ethnic matching occur across as well as within racial, social, economic, and other diversity groupings? What are the most salient attributes of effective student-teacher ethnic matching? This book requires engaged reading and deep understanding of its associated issues if these questions are to be addressed adequately and the potential of ethnic matching is fully realized.

Readers should think broadly about the meanings and manifestations of ethnic matching between teachers and students of color and how this idea is related to race consciousness and cultural responsiveness in improving these students' school achievement. Also, nuanced differences between race and ethnicity presented in this book, and how they are interconnected in US education past and present, should be examined carefully. While ethnicity and race are closely related, they are not synonymous. One is primarily sociological, and the other is physiological. Ethnicity commonly refers to cultural traits of large social groups.

However, there is diversity within ethnic groups. Race generally refers to physical characteristics, but the value assessments and quality of interactions associated with them are socially constructed. An ethnic group can be comprised of many different races, and a race can include many different ethnicities. Thus, equating ethnic matching with only race-based similarities is inaccurate, since it is possible for people to be racially similar but ethnically different. As Easton-Brooks cautions, teachers who share racial identities with their students are not automatically and effectively ethnically matched with them. Race similarity may increase the probability of ethnic matching but does not guarantee it.

Therefore, it is likely for Black teachers to be ethnically matched with Black students, Latinx teachers with Latinx students, and Navajo teachers with Navajo students. Yet all Black, Latinx, and Navajo teachers will not necessarily be good ethnic matches for all students of their respective ethnic and racial groups. Sure, race is a factor in the ethnic matching matrix, but other social attributes and competencies are imperative too, such as levels of ethnic affinity and identity, cultural consciousness, social class, economic status, residential location, and culturally responsive pedagogical competence.

It is not so important for students and teachers to be members of the same racial groups. Instead, it is important for teachers to have the knowledge, skills, and will to incorporate culturally diverse content, points of reference, and styles of learning in their personal and pedagogical interactions with ethnically diverse students to enhance their academic and other kinds of achievement. A recent example of this kind of ethnic matching was reported in the June 30, 2018, edition of the *Seattle Times*.

The graduation of two family doctors trained in the residency program of the Seattle Indian Health Board was celebrated in the cultural traditions of Native Americans. Rather than the graduates being given futuristic expectations of service and success rendered by a renowned speaker and wearing the traditional mainstream mortarboards, they participated in a spiritual ceremony that involved being wrapped in Native songs, blessings, and blankets. In this instance the symbols of success were culturally consistent with the location (the Indian Health Board) of study, the participating "students" (although one of the two graduates was not Native American but had been immersed in an indigenous-based cultural educational program), and the constituents they were prepared to serve. Consequently, ethnic matching occurred on multiple levels. In responding to these cultural rituals one of the graduates declared, "Representation matters." This is a key message conveyed through ethnic matching.

If ethnic matching were analogous to race-based matching it would not be feasible, given the racial-numerical disparities between students and teachers in US schools and colleges. As Easton-Brooks points out graphically, there simply are not enough teachers of color to physically match with all students of color. Even though these numerical gaps are described in detail, they are still somewhat deceptive because membership in an ethnic group does not guarantee identity and affiliation. Fortunately, ethnic and cultural knowledge, respect, and skills of engagement can be learned by both in- and out-group members.

This cultural knowledge and congruency in teaching and learning can compensate for numerical racial imbalances. The author of this book places the onus for developing the attitudes, values, knowledge, and skills necessary for implementing ethnic matching on teacher preservice education and in-service professional development. This teacher learning should include understanding racial distinctions and inequities in educational opportunities and society at large and culturally responsiveness as a body of methodological procedures for improving the performance of students of color from different ethnic backgrounds.

Although its dynamics and complexity may make ethnic matching difficult to achieve in practice, the benefits, according to Easton-Brooks, are worth the challenges. He is not alone in this endorsement. Many scholars (among them, Endim, 2016; Hammond, 2015; Ladson-Billings, 2009; Park & Walberg, 2007) from different disciplines and perspectives agree and extend the benefits to include positive results beyond academics, such as stronger cultural identity and sustainability; better interpersonal relationships across ethnic, racial, and cultural differences; and more engaged and productive citizenship.

In other words, effective ethnic matching generates *improved holistic performance for diverse students*. Its value anchors and behavioral guidelines are deep knowledge, respect, and application of various forms of cultural diversity. Thus, the essence of ethnic matching as explained in this book is contingent upon a multiplicity of cross-cultural competencies. These competencies are the results of learning and not biological inheritance.

Consequently, teachers from any ethnic group can potentially be ethnically matched with students from other ethnic groups. This possibility is still more ideal than real, due in part to the sporadic and often superficial study of cultural, racial, and ethnic diversity in the professional preparation of educators and the continuing absence of substantive and sustained interracial, interethnic, and cross-cultural interactions in US society at large.

Thus, in actual practice ethnic matching is likely to be more attainable among students and teachers who are members of the same racial categories or living conditions (such as immigrants from specific countries, linguistic and cultural backgrounds; victims of oppression, discrimination, and marginalization), but this is not a mandatory condition.

This may be why throughout the book Easton-Brooks makes frequent references to ethnic matching between teachers of students of color and is deliberate about helping readers to understand essential culturally diverse knowledge and skills teachers need to acquire, their potential for effecting positive effects on student achievement, and some of the challenges provoked by the ideas and actions of ethnic matching. In promoting these mandates, he joins other scholars such as McCarty and Lee (2014), Gasman and Tudico (2008), and Ybarra (1998).

Contrary to the tendencies of many in pursuit of effective educational endeavors for students of color to concentrate primarily on the products of practice, the focus in this volume is on the *processes* of ethnic matching—that is, what they look like behaviorally, not just ideologically, or the effects they produce. For example, if empathy, trust, and respectful relationships filtered through cultural diversity are fundamental values of ethnic matching, the emphasis is on how they are actualized in practice and to what effect for both students and teachers.

It makes pragmatic and pedagogical sense for authors to use constituencies they know best (whether from lived experiences or academic study) when translating their conceptual and theoretical ideas into actual practices. Given the emphasis Easton-Brooks places on Blacks specifically and students of color generally, one can deduce that these are his primary targets of concern and advocacy. Readers should not chastise or criticize him for these focused concentrations or deny him the right to choose.

Instead, they should appreciate why and how the use of particular people, situations, and contexts crystallizes the meaning of the general idea of ethnic matching. By mixing general ideas and specific actions this book demonstrates how to blend theory and practice as compiled from research, scholarship, and the personal experiences of practicing classroom teachers. The combination of these diverse data sets provides further validation of the proposal (i.e., ethnic matching) and heightens its credibility by offering multiple perspectives from diversified educators and places or locations within the educational enterprise.

These multiple perspectives, ways of engaging in ethnic matching, and the effects they generate should be inviting and enticing for others to join the cause. They certainly exemplify another key component of the concept—that is, using multiple methods to achieve intended learning outcomes for students of color that are more consistent with their experiential and cultural backgrounds. Consequently, there is much needed modeling and mentoring in this book for preparing teachers to use and facilitate ethnic matching with their racially, socially, ethnically, culturally, and linguistically diverse students.

Also in this book, teachers are strongly encouraged to be self-knowledgeable and self-reflective "in the moment" of their behavioral occurrences. Easton-Brooks demonstrates this powerfully by juxtaposing "stories" of actual teaching behaviors with theorized or conceptualized notions about being culturally knowledgeable, conscious, and responsive in teaching students of color. In other words, he engages in interpretative reflection on the descriptions of teaching behaviors *as a habit of being* that is fundamental to effective ethnic matching in teaching and learning.

These "stories" are multisourced and multidirectional. They come from different perspectives, people, contexts, and locations in the educational enterprise. This diversity adds credence to the validity of ethnic matching and increases its appeal and applicability as a method worthy of pursuit in moving educational equity from mystery to mandate, from idea to action, and from possibility to reality. *Ethnic Matching: Academic Success of Students of Color* helps to facilitate these transitions and transformations for students of color.

It also recognizes, without equivocation, that many teachers of color exhibit instructional attitudes, values, and skills worthy of emulation in improving the educational opportunities and outcomes across many manifestations of diversity among students. That is, they *do* ethnic matching! More teachers from different racial, ethnic, and cultural identities must learn to do likewise to better serve the education needs of racially diverse students in US schools.

Geneva L. Gay
University of Washington–Seattle

REFERENCES

Ashley, D., Williams, J., & Ingrum, A. (2009). *I'll find a way or make one: A tribute to historically Black colleges and universities*. New York: Harper Collins.

Dembski, B., & Thomas, A. (2016). *It takes* ganas: *Jaime Escalante's secret to inspired learning*. Ecorys, UK: Erasmus Press.

Endim, C. (2016). *For White folks who teach in the hood . . . and the rest of y'all too: Reality pedagogy and urban education*. Boston, MA: Beacon Press.

Fleming, J. (1991). *Blacks in college: A comparative study of students' success in Black and White institutions*. San Francisco, CA: Jossey-Bass.

Foster, M. (1997). *Black teachers on teaching*. New York: The New Press.

Gasman, M., & Tudico, C. L. (Eds.). (2008). *Historically Black colleges and universities: Triumphs, troubles, and taboos.* New York: Palgrave Macmillan.

Hammond, Z. L. (2015). *Culturally responsive teaching and the brain: Promoting authentic engagement and rigor among culturally and linguistically diverse students.* Thousand Oaks, CA: Corwin.

Ladson-Billings, G. (2009). *The dreamkeepers: Successful teachers for African American children* (2nd ed.). San Francisco, CA: Jossey-Bass.

Mathews, J. (1989). *Escalante: The best teacher in America.* New York: Holt.

McCarty, T. L., & Lee, T. S. (2014). Critical culturally sustaining/revitalizing pedagogy and indigenous education sovereignty. *Harvard Educational Review, 84*(1), 101–124.

Park, S. J., & Walberg, H. J. (2007). *Narrowing the achievement gap: Strategies for educating Latino, Black, and Asian students.* New York: Springer Science and Business Med.

Siddle Walker, V. (1996). *Their highest potential: An African American school community in the segregated South.* New York: Teachers College Press.

Ybarra, R. (1998). *Educating Latino students: A guide for successful practices.* Lancaster, PA: Technomic Publishing Company.

Preface

WHERE DO WE START?

As we go through life, we go through it with a set of assumptions about the world, the way it exists, or the way we wish for it to exist. Thus, we sculpt a worldview that is limited to our unique set of experiences. However, at some point, each of us, if we think critically about our worldviews, recognizes that our own reality is more insular than we once believed. These revelations occur when we ask *critical questions*—inquiries that admit the possibility of a truth unlike the assumptions we have always held. It isn't until we consider and investigate these critical questions that we open ourselves up to seeing the world as it is rather than as we have narrowly imagined it.

I began asking critical questions about education when I left my hometown. I grew up in a Black neighborhood in Houston, Texas. There, everything that existed to me centered on Blackness and Black culture. As I left this safety net to explore the world, my assumption was that the world would mirror and function much like my Kashmere Gardens neighborhood of Houston, the only world I had known. It wasn't until I entered college that I started challenging that reality with critical questions. I was awakened quickly to a different existence, and the world has never looked the same since.

As an academic, I have been intently interested in factors impacting the academic lives of students of color. The interest, admittedly, comes from my experience as a public school student growing up in Houston in the '70s and '80s. Through my public school career, most of my teachers were Black. I can remember having maybe five White teachers from PK to grade 12. I assumed this was the norm. I believed that the teaching profession was a commonplace for Blacks.

I also thought that Mexican teachers taught Mexican students, White teachers taught White students, and so on. It was not until I taught in the Denver area in the '90s that I realized that my beliefs bore little resemblance to reality. In my first school, I was the only teacher of color and the only male in the elementary building. I thought, "Where are all the teachers of color?" It was the first of many critical questions that challenged my childhood ignorance and initiated my journey investigating the intersection of race, culture, and education.

Granted, at the time, Denver was not the multicultural mecca of the world or nearly as diverse as it currently is. However, and when pulling from my old frame of reference, I was shocked there were not more people of color in the education profession. I could no longer maintain that Mexican teachers taught Mexican students and White teachers taught White students; rather, I felt compelled to ask the critical questions that would provide me with an accurate, albeit unsettling, understanding of public education.

As I matured in the profession and directed my professional path toward research and graduate-level studies, I learned that students of color were not performing academically as successfully as White students on any level; again, this did not match my preconceived ideas of the educational system. Furthermore, I realized quickly just by looking around that the field of education was not diverse.

So, in my master's program and later through my doctoral studies, I focused on studying and understanding the deeper historical, sociocultural, and political movements in the US educational system that led to such different experiences between my time in public school as a student in one context and my experience as a teacher in another. Fast-forwarding a few years, as I became a professor and a researcher, I started presenting at conferences and engaging in other forms of scholarship. Through these experiences, I started coming into contact with people who went to school in my neighborhood.

After meeting four people from my neighborhood or adjacent neighborhoods with doctoral degrees, I wondered about the commonalities among us. What I found that we shared was that the majority of our teachers were Black. This led me to explore "ethnic matching," to better understand students of color who had experiences with teachers of color: Could this factor improve the academic outcomes of students of color?[1] Through my research, I found the idea to be true.

MOTIVATION

Along the way of writing this book, I lost two of the most impactful men in my life: my Uncle William (Bill) Ray Brooks and his brother and my father,

Isaac Ray Brooks. While this made completing the book challenging, it was the pride and belief they had in me that gave me the strength to do so. Some of my last memories with and of them were back in their hometown of Shady Grove, Louisiana, in Natchitoches Parish. It was at my Uncle Bill's funeral that my father shared with me—at a point I could hear it—his life and educational experience growing up as a Black kid in Louisiana, pre–Civil Rights.

Here he explained how his father lost the land he owned and farmed for years because Whites wanted the land. Because he would not sell, taxes were raised to the point that my grandfather and other Blacks lost their land because they could not afford the taxes. Here is also where he shared the story of my Uncle Bill, who as a teen killed a White man in self-defense yet had to go to prison for murdering that White man.

Before the passing of Uncle Bill and my father, roughly six months later, they had shared with me the story of my great-great grandmother, a house slave who had a son (Sam Sowell) by her owner. Given that she was a slave, her name and humanity were lost. However, before the death of my uncle and father, I was able to find the name of my great-great grandmother, Ciley, or Kizzie. This discovery felt good because we were now able to humanize a dear family member.

Because of these experiences, I feel it is important to continue pushing toward reducing inequitable systems that challenge us, stress us, dehumanize us, and make it difficult to bask in the sunlight of opportunity.

Acknowledgments

Before we can set our sights on the future, it is very important that we honor those who have come before us. They are the pioneers who met the challenges and made it easier for us to do our work as we set the path for a new generation. To this end I would like to acknowledge Sarah Roberts and her family, who first attempted to break down barriers of inequity in 1848, as Boston Public Schools would not let her attend a local school in her neighborhood. While slavery still existed in southern states, imagine the courage it took for this Black family to sue Boston Public Schools during this era.

Then, just over one hundred years later, Linda Brown and her family—this time with success—broke down the barriers of inequity in the famous *Brown v. The Board of Education* case, in 1954. During the years between these two cases, many Blacks and others have fought to gain equitable educational opportunities. So, along with Sarah Roberts and Linda Brown, I would like to acknowledge the many relocated First Nations people, Latinx, Asian subgroups, and other groups continuing to pursue educational equity; and the heroes of civil rights in education, such as Malala Yousafzai, Charles Hamilton Houston, W. E. B. Du Bois, Barbara Jordan, Thurgood Marshall, the Little Rock Nine, and the many other pioneers of color who publicly challenged educational systems.

In addition, I would like to thank many of my colleagues, with whom I have shared conversations, debates, and critical dialogues about this book. These interactions helped me to shape the book's direction and conversation and forced me to apply a realistic approach to it, whether I agreed with their "realities" or not.

Chapter 1

Framework of the Book

In this book, my research and that of others will help readers better understand the impact teachers of color have on the lives of students of color. This approach is meant to lend support to the field as a whole, to teachers of all races and ethnicities, on how to interact with students of color through key practices and beliefs, to assist in increasing the academic success of these students.

There is no dearth of research concerning how to positively impact the academic and socioemotional outcomes of students of color—and all students, for that matter. Some of the work that has been produced, admittedly, is not so approachable to those who most need it. It is necessary to frame that work, much of which is quantitative.

Before continuing, there should first be an understanding of the landscape of our country and our public schools to help us better understand the need to learn about effective ways of teaching students of color. Since the turn of this century, the United States has witnessed considerable growth in its ethnic/racial minority populations, to the point that we must consider whether the concept "minority" is a relevant term on many levels.

For instance, the rate of growth of the Asian/Pacific Islander, Latinx, Native American/First Nations, and Black populations has notably surpassed the growth rate of Whites between 1980 and 2005. The Asian/Pacific Islander and Latinx populations increased at a substantial rate compared to other US ethnic groups. There was considerable growth in the First Nations/Native population. Blacks grew moderately, while there was little growth among the White population. Therefore, the concept "minority" is becoming less relevant when speaking of people of color, because it is predicted that the growth in the "minority" population will continue to surpass that of Whites.

If it can be accepted that this is real, as one is inclined to do, then perhaps what is necessary is a retheorizing of the concepts of minority/majority and White/people of color. Perhaps the retheorizing must go beyond conventional dialectics that reify group conflict rather than work to understand and incorporate the heterogeneity and variation that are happening so quickly within and between groups. If education is a domain for the promotion of social justice, it is perhaps time to consider the meaning and usage of the commonplace terms used to talk about the injustices.

POPULATION CHANGE IN THE UNITED STATES

By 2060, the Asian/Pacific Islanders, Latinx, and First Nations populations are anticipated to impressively exceed the European American/White and Black populations. While the percentage of Blacks will diminish, this does not mean there will be fewer Blacks in the United States. This only demonstrates that Blacks—and Whites, for that matter—won't develop at an indistinguishably fast rate from the other US ethnic groups.

If these projections hold, people of color will make up 57 percent of the US population by 2060. We as of now observe this pattern in states like Hawaii, New Mexico, California, and Texas, where non-Hispanic Whites make up just over 50 percent of the population. Further, it is projected that by 2060, there will be no one group that has a "majority" share of the total US population. Though not within the scope of this work, what we might find is that our language for categorization might have to change soon and become more relevant.

As the US ethnic makeup changes, again, we must consider if the concept "minority" is a relevant concept. Let's take it a step further. The concept "minority" on some levels can be suggestive. For starters, it is a concept dichotomous in nature. One is either a "minority" or "White." However, what has been historically suggested by the term "minority" is that one is either Black or Mexican. The concept has historically negated, in use, the recognition of all other ethnic people of color and is hardly sensitive to biracial coupling. Nevertheless, the concept, like many dichotomous concepts, suggests us versus them, or a valuable versus invaluable mindset.

One has to admit that the concept "minority" is a term that was not there in the past. The term came to be used as a representation of people of color. It was not until others used the concept that its power, unintended or not, was first thought of. Traditionally, "minority" or "ethnic minority" played a critical role in determining laws. It suggests that those in "power," socially, economically, and so forth, are the majority.

For instance, when considering groups in relation to gender, males are thought of as the majority and females as the minority when, in fact, there are more females than males in the United States. This thinking comes from the positions of power males hold in the United States. Within this context, the term "minority" can hold to being powerless. Many times, when the term "minority" is used, it is not meant to suggest people who are power-less. However, its historical use can seem to suggest a "powerless group of people."

On a global level, the term "minority" has different meanings. In many other countries it often refers to "linguistic minorities" (i.e., those who speak another language), while in the United States it often refers to race/ethnicity. However, the United States is just as diverse in language as we are in race/ethnicity. Different from the United States, though, countries such as Canada, China, Germany, India, the United Kingdom, and Ethiopia allow those with different native languages to interact with government and be educated in their mother tongue.

There are other reasons, which are outside the scope of this book, that point to why "minority" is not truly representative of "people of color." In one of the first uses of the concept "people of color" in the early 1800s, the concept described anyone with at least a drop of "Black blood" as a person of color.[1] Again, the concept "people of color" was first used to dichotomize two groups of people (i.e., Black and White). Today, this concept is broader and represents the commonalities of non-White ethnic groups in the United States. So, in this book, "people of color" rather than "minorities" has been and will be used as a proxy for non-Whites.

DEMOGRAPHY SHIFT IN US PUBLIC SCHOOLS

Even more significantly, the term "minority" is becoming less relevant in describing students of color in public schools. Just as we see the national landscape changing, our public schools are becoming less White at an even faster rate. For instance, the students of color population in US public schools increased by 73 percent while that of the White students decreased by 2 percent.

Additionally, between 2003 and 2013, we have seen the White public school population decline from 59 percent to 50 percent of the total. In 2013, Whites made up less than 50 percent of the public school student body in Southern and Western states. In Southern states, the makeup was 45 percent White, 24 percent Black, and 24 percent Latinx. In Western states, the composition was 39 percent White, 42 percent Latinx, and 9 percent Asian.

Meanwhile, in schools in the Northeast and Midwest, the White student populations were much larger than that of students of color.

However, in both regions, the student-of-color population has increased by at least 11 percent since 1995. On a national level, if these rates of growth continue, students of color will make up roughly 55 percent of the public school population by 2025. When we further examine this transformation in public schools, we find some schools are already seeing a drastic change in their population. For example, Houston Independent School District (HISD), the seventh largest school district in the country, consists of 62 percent Latinx, 26 percent Black, 8 percent White, and 3 percent Asian. The most common languages in the district are Arabic, Vietnamese, Mandarin Chinese, Nepali, and Urdu.

Many of the largest school districts, like New York City Schools, Los Angeles Unified School District, Chicago Public Schools, and Miami-Dade County Public Schools, vary in the breakdown of their student population. However, what is constant among these districts is that students of color make up 80 to 90 percent of their student population. This phenomenon is not just impacting urban schools. Smaller communities are also seeing a change in their student population. For instance, many of the rural schools in eastern Oregon have students of color making up anywhere from 50 to 70 percent of their student population.

Furthermore, the state of Oregon as a whole has seen its student population of color increase 20 percent since 1996, and the third highest growth in the country between 2003 to 2013. Even predominantly White states like South Dakota, Minnesota, Iowa, and Maine have seen the population of their students of color grow 8 to 10 percent over a ten-year span. The school district in Sioux Falls, the largest city in South Dakota, now has 33 percent students of color.

While we are experiencing a population shift both in society and in our public schools, we have yet to master a collective successful academic system for many of our students of color. Data from the 2013 National Report Card continue to show a gap in the academic achievement scores of students of color compared to White students.

For instance, White students continue to outperform Black, Latinx, and First Nations/Native American students in twelfth-grade mathematics test scores. Although mathematics achievement scores are not the only way or perhaps not the best way to measure academic success, it is still a measure that demonstrates the difference in educational outcomes for students. Even when considering if students complete high school or graduate from college, there is still a significant difference in the mathematics achievement scores between Blacks and Whites and Latinx and White students.

When assessing the difference in mathematics achievement scores of twelfth graders within groups, there is a distinction in the math achievement scores between those who graduate from high school and those who do not, and between those who graduate from college and those who do not. However, among Black and Latinx students, there is no real distinction in math scores between those who graduate from high school and those who do not, and between those who graduate from college and those who do not.

SCHOOLS ARE MORE THAN BLACK, WHITE, AND LATINX

Of interest is that Asian students outperformed White students in grade 12 math testing. However, a group of Asian professionals who were part of the Washington Office of Superintendent of Public Instruction's Ethnic Think Tank proposed that it is wrong to assume that all Asians perform the same. As John Ogbu suggested, how a group of people responds to an educational system is a direct reflection of how the group members feel their society/community responds to them.[2]

There are more than sixteen Asian groups in the Seattle area. There are hidden academic opportunity gaps among Asian Americans and Pacific Islanders according to the disaggregated data from Washington State and the National Commission on Asian American and Pacific Islander Research in Education.[3] The group felt that the scores might not have reflected much smaller Asian groups such as Cambodians, Vietnamese, Hmong, and others. For instance, when you look at Limited English Proficiency (LEP) in Washington State, the average among the Asian population was 39.5 percent in 2000.[4]

However, Japanese (24 percent) and Asian Indians (25.2 percent) were well below that average of Asian Americans in Washington State.[5] On the other hand, Vietnamese (65.6 percent) and Hmong (65.5 percent) were well above the average. Further, Seattle Public Schools showed a discrepancy in tenth-grade mathematics scores between the different Asian groups in 2007–2008.

The data showed Chinese, Japanese, and Korean students scoring well above the average among Asian students, and Cambodians, Hmong, Mien, and other Laotian students scoring nearly 18 percent below the average among Asian students in Seattle Public Schools.

The point is that we have to be careful not to assume all Asian ethnic groups perform at the same level; there are social, economic, language, and other factors that may impact the academic performance of these students.

As opposed to Washington State, Minnesota at one point grouped all of its Black population together; and the state consistently speaks of having the second largest Black/White achievement gap in the country. However, the state's Black population comprises three distinct Black groups: Somali refugees—40 percent of the total US Somali refugees live in Minnesota; Ethiopians; and Blacks who migrated from mainly the South and Chicago and who have no identification with recent Black immigrant groups.

The challenge facing Minnesota is that the data aggregate all Black groups together and does not take into account the language differences that can impact the academic outcomes of the immigrant Blacks versus the nonimmigrant Blacks. For instance, 15 percent of Ethiopians and 18 percent of Somali are reported not to speak English well or at all at age five or higher. In comparison, Blacks who are not immigrants did not fall into this category.

What can be seen as a systemic problem is that while there is growth among ethnic groups beyond Whites both in the country in general and in our public schools, we have yet to conquer the development of an overall educational system that responds to students of color. There have been several approaches, policies, practices, and research on strategies designed to help students of color become more academically successful. Of these approaches, practice and research have clearly shown a greater continuity between the home culture and school culture of students of color contributing to the academic success of these populations.

SYSTEMS, CHALLENGES, AND SOLUTIONS

The challenge schools face is how to replicate home culture at school while at the same time responding to the needs of all students. As an alternative, many preservice and service teachers have engaged in multicultural education and culturally responsive practice to interact with students on a cultural level. However, while there is evidence this approach works, the academic success of students of color is still minimal.

It may be that while teachers are engaging in culturally responsive training, the authentic connection between school culture and home culture is not quite present. So the question is, how do we create an authentic experience between teachers/schools and students of color while educating all students? Much of this book is dedicated to helping answer this question. What we know from research, including my own research, is that if students of color interact with teachers of color in an academic setting, the academic success of students of color increases significantly compared to students of color who do not interact with teachers of color.[6]

The author conducted two major studies with colleagues looking at the effects of Black teachers on the reading and mathematics scores of Black students over their elementary school experience. In both studies, we used a national representative sample to examine the long-term effects on reading scores in one study and mathematics scores in another study on Black students who were matched/paired with a Black teacher between kindergarten and fifth grade.

In both cases, we found that Black students performed better in kindergarten when paired with a Black teacher than did Black students who weren't paired with a Black teacher. Further, we found that if Black students had at least one Black teacher between kindergarten and fifth grades, the growth in their reading and mathematics scores were greater than for Black students who did not have a Black teacher between kindergarten and fifth grades. More details about these students will be given in chapter 2.

Similar studies have shown similar results.[7] Also, when exploring ethnic matching among Latinx students, Beatriz Clewell and colleagues found an increase in the reading and mathematics scores of Black and Latinx elementary students in the fourth and sixth grades when they were taught by a teacher of the same ethnicity.[8] Scholars have discussed why my findings and those of my colleagues and others have quantifiably demonstrated that when matched with a teacher of color, students of color will show significant academic achievement.

Scholars have shown there is a strong association between culture and knowledge in relation to teachers of color when linked to the teaching and instructional practices geared toward students of color.[9] This book will share the particulars on the rationale on why these findings are valuable and important to increasing the academic outcomes of students of color. Through this work, studies have shown that students of color are seen differently by Black teachers than by White teachers.

These findings and the findings above are not meant to suggest that if schools simply hire teachers of color to work directly with students of color, the academic performance of students of color will be resolved. Instead, the findings presented here show that students of color tend to do better academically when they engage with teachers of color. The question is, why?

Also, this book does not mean to imply that all teachers of color are effective in working with students of color. There are teachers in the category who are not qualified nor well trained nor well prepared who may maintain a deficit mindset with regard to these students. This book will demonstrate the difference between those teachers and teachers of color who are truly impactful when working with students of color.

Further, the field is also finding both students of color and White students had a more favorable perception of Latinx and Black teachers than they did of White teachers.[10] These findings along with the other cited findings aim to support the need for a more diverse teacher workforce as well as the need to understand the attributes teachers of color have that encourage the success of students.

This book presents the idea that as the US population shifts, the challenge for public schools is in creating an academic environment that is more successful for students of color and that teachers of color can increase the academic success of students of color. However, while we need to work on diversifying the education workforce, it is unrealistic to think this solution alone will solve the academic needs of students of color. What this book is looking to suggest is that by understanding the attributes/practices teachers of color bring to the table, we can better understand and act on the needs of students of color in the classroom through training, managing the schools, and also through policies.

It is important for me to note that this book is not about providing step-by-step guidelines on how to work with students of color. The reason is that we are not machines that all respond the same to every situation. We are humans, and we respond to situations based on a number of factors and mostly from a cultural and cultural-historical lens. Therefore, this book is not about limiting the cultural elements that teachers bring to the profession. This book serves more to provide insight into what successful teachers of color bring to the profession, in the hope that we can help shape the understanding of what it takes to assist in helping students of color to succeed.

Chapter 2

Ethnic Matching as a Concept

I teach because I truly believe that education is our greatest hope as a crumbling society. I am in love with learning. I recognize the flaws in the traditional education system, but I do not believe that our system is beyond saving. Through the ingenuity of educators and the resilience of our youth, education can be the saving grace of society. I'm passionate about equity and providing opportunities for young people to have a voice in their own education. We don't learn unless we participate in our learning. And that is why I teach.

—*Native Spanish-speaking teacher from California*

What is ethnic matching? The concept refers to the pairing of a person receiving a service from a professional in which the two share the same race/ethnicity. An example of this would be pairing a client with a therapist of the same race/ethnicity, a student with a teacher of the same race/ethnicity, or a patient with a doctor of the same race/ethnicity. While this concept has not been defined in the literature, the framework of ethnic matching has been proposed as a practice in the literature for the past few decades.

In practice, ethnic matching has been used in human resources, management, and supervision, and more recently, in higher education, counseling, and teacher education. The results of ethnic matching in these areas produce stronger recovery from mental health issues, better job satisfaction, stronger college retention, and higher academic achievement. The results are witnessed across both whites and people of color. The concept has also been used globally in research and practice. So what does ethnic matching suggest?

DEVELOPING PERCEPTIVE KNOWLEDGE

It is hard to believe that people are so mentally or psychologically segregated that for them to feel productive or motivated, they should be matched with someone of their same ethnicity or race for society to function effectively. While research would support that sometimes this may be the case, it is important to understand how this may occur. Ultimately, people come into experiences or interactions with a frame of reference.

Let's take for instance a child entering grade school for the first time. This child brings in a wealth of experience with *hir*[1,2] from the past five years or so. The child's experience and frame of reference about school, teachers, and other students can be centered on the child's prior experience in preschool. If the child never attended preschool, the frame of reference associated with schooling is more or less based on the child's idea of schooling. Either way, what the child brings to the experience is very real and will be the framework on which *ze* future experiences will be based.

Let's put this child's experience in greater perspective. This child is bringing in five years of experience based on cultural factors, family structure and function, community, and other factors related to that child's environment. Let's take it a step further. If someone has five years of work experience in the same field, one might believe this person has strong knowledge or experience in that field. In the same way, this child has five years of experience, again, centered on those factors in that child's cultural surroundings.

Therefore, the child's frame of reference will help *hir* in connecting experienced situations or interactions with something that *ze* can mentally make sense of based on past experiences.[3] Neurologically, this is a matter of connecting synapses, simply linking new experiences to existing memories in the brain. What drives this connection or allows this connection to occur is based on how well the child can relate new experiences with existing memories or knowledge relevantly similar to that which is being experienced. Importantly, how and why this connection is made need not make sense to outsiders. The experience merely has to make sense to the person making the connection.[4]

For instance, consider the classic study of little Albert and the white rat, in which Albert was presented with a white rat and every time he went to touch the rat, researchers would make a loud noise behind him. This created in the child's mind a memory of fear in association with the white rat. Therefore, every time the child was presented with something that looked similar to the white rat, the child would become distressed. In the child's mind, this made perfect sense, but to an outsider who had no association with the experience of the child, this might not have the same level of relevance.

Here, others may be able at some level to understand why the child's reaction occurs; yet they may also see the disassociation between the experiences. However, once these connections are embedded into memory either at the conscious or subconscious level, the assimilation of this experience and existing memory becomes the framework for which rational thinking transpires. Critical to this process is not just having an experience that creates memory but what transfers this experience into memory as well.

A sociological framework could argue that memories are not confirmed as working memories (e.g., knowledge) until the perception of the experience is mentally confirmed through some negotiated social experience(s). The suggestion here is that memory exists in the subconscious, but how others react to the person's response to the situation can hold weight in how a person internalizes the situation to memory.

With little Albert, how the adults around him reacted to the sound and the white rat could have helped reshape this experience for him. Let's say that the adults around him reacted with joy, excitement, or with cheers when the loud noise was made. Could this have given Albert a different memory or framework related to this experience?

Now let's take that child who enters school for the first time. This approach suggests that for the child to build memory, knowledge, or a perception of a situation or interaction this child first attempts to mentally relate this experience to something the child has experienced before. This becomes the child's perceived knowledge of a situation, an experience, or information that refers to making sense of new information but has yet to be tested through some negotiated social interaction. Again, the perceived knowledge is real and relevant to the individual and that individual's prior experience(s).

Next, what makes this perceptive knowledge real to the individual is how others respond to the way the individual sees the situation through either direct or indirect interactions. However, what often confirms the person's perceptive knowledge of a situation is based on that person's socioenvironmental factors, such as cultural influences, race/ethnic influences, gender influences, economic status, and so on. These factors act as reference points for an individual as these have strong impacts on the social and intellectual framework of the individual.

Therefore, a person's beliefs and perceptive knowledge becomes the building block from which all other knowledge and experiences will be measured. From a social neuroscientific view, social interactions can be critical in making sense of a situation. Simply put, people are naturally social animals and rely on social interactions to help in navigating and making sense of the world. Therefore, social interactions are necessary for the brain to internalize the meaning of experiences, situations, or learning in general.

Simple things like facial expressions, gestures, movements, vocal tones, and other physical characteristics can influence the way a person cognitively processes knowledge. However, when the external cues (i.e., physical gestures, etc.) don't match or show no similarity to previous knowledge, this can lead to confusion or *social stress*, which refers to the anxiety or discomfort a person feels when interacting with others.[5] It should not be mistaken that social stress results from a person's lack of social capital, emotional intelligence, or social competence.

As these factors can influence social stress, they can also contribute to a difference in expectation or understanding of an interaction, experience, or information presented to an individual. Let's take for instance the child from a cultural community in which facial expressions and hand gestures are a significant part of communication, especially when expressing excitement or frustration. While these forms of communication are not meant to display aggression, these cues are merely forms of cultural communication.

Given this, an example would be a child entering a situation in which an adult expresses frustration or disappointment in a choice the child had made. However, the adult showed little to no emotional facial expression or hand gestures. From the child's prior experience or mentally processed information on what adult frustration looks like, there may be a disconnect for the child between what the adult is saying and what the adult is physically displaying. Therefore, the child may be unable to adapt or will become perplexed in trying to make sense of this interaction.

This situation can also happen in reverse, meaning a child could be from a cultural setting in which little or no expression is given and yet experience an adult from a cultural setting in which facial expressions and gestures are a big part of that person's communication style. This can also exist in adult-to-adult interactions. In either case, one or the other can be perceived as being aggressive or passive, when in actuality that is not the case.

If such an interaction is repeated with no cues to assist the child or individual in understanding or coping with this situation, this could also lead to *mental stress*. This type of stress affects chemical balances and neurological function and can impact the individual's speech, ability to process information, or ability to perform simple tasks. Again, let's go back to little Albert. Given that no one negotiated, or helped him make sense of, the association between the noise and the white rat, the repetition of this interaction may have caused Albert both social and mental stress.

Another impact of the social neuro process happens when individuals are using interactions or conversations to help understand a situation, experience, or learning but are not feeling heard or seen as relevant. This can also increase or create stress, which can lead to low self-esteem and undesired behaviors as a result of frustration. But another way to look at this is through the lens of *cultural dissonance*, which refers to a sort of cultural clash in which an individual struggles to mentally make sense of a cultural occurrence.

An individual can experience cultural dissonance through cultural change that creates a sense of disharmony, confusion, or conflict. Let's take for instance a first- or second-generation immigrant entering school in a new country. As the individual enters school, the person can experience changes that are culturally unexpected and unexplained—dissonance itself. Dissonance implies that there is inconsistency in a person's perception of an experience or situation, between what an individual believes or expects from a situation versus a confusing thought or set of thoughts that are generated by the situation. When culture is a factor, this suggests there is possibly a cultural disruption or clash for the individual, which must be resolved to allow the individual to make sense of this disruption and come to some level of mental adaption.

For a person to function within a setting in which dissonance or disequilibrium exists, the person's basic survivor mode is to come to a state of harmony or understanding. In this process, the person either (1) adjusts *hir* way of thinking to cope with this challenging experience, (2) changes *hir* reaction to the experience to help one calm *hirself*, or (3) reconceptualizes the situation as a way of rethinking the experience. For little Albert, this means he could (1) think that the loud noise is not that bad or normal, (2) simply move away from the sound upon hearing the sound, or (3) reconceptualize the situation through rationality, thinking, for example, given that no one else is scared or bothered by the noises, there is no need for him to fear the noise.

In this case or on a cultural rim, the challenge here is that the individual could be left feeling devalued, given that none of the adults attempted to help resolve the situation, and/or left feeling confused as to whether the choice the individual made about the situation was a valid way to handle it. While the individual may have a way of coping with the situation, the individual's level of social or mental stress is not reduced—unless of course the individual is very resilient and does not let these types of stress bother *hir*.

However, resilience or even finding one of the three ways to mentally cope with cultural dissonance can only occur if the individual feels that *ze* had a choice in the matter. For instance, as an immigrant child enters a schoolroom with no other cultural frame of reference, the person can be left to believe that *hir* cultural values are less relevant in the classroom, again, leading to mental or social stress.

Stress can also occur once a child is engaged in a classroom in which all of *hir* beliefs are viewed as false because the beliefs of the teacher, one of power, or the majority of others is in direct disagreement with *hir* experiences. Take, for instance, a person who grew up in an all-Black neighborhood where US history was taught from a Black perspective entering a US history course in college, where what is taught is in contrast with the way *ze* understood history in association with Blacks. The choice here is to change one's way of thinking or accept the consequences for not adjusting *hir* way of thinking about the topic.

Again, this could lead to mental and social stress as well as a sense of feeling devalued in the classroom and possibly the school. Therefore, the structure of developing perceptive knowledge can look very biased, and often it is bias based on whom the individual socializes with. Individuals often limit their interactions mainly to those with similar or common cultures, experiences, values, or beliefs (e.g., religion, politics, ethnic culture, etc.). Rarely does an individual look for diverse experiences to help shape the individual's perceived knowledge of a situation.

A person tends to place more value on those who share the same truth about the world and the way it functions than on those who do not necessarily share their same truth. This happens either by choice or by circumstance. For instance, when experiences associated with race arise, people tend to talk about such experiences with others of the same race or with others who share their values about race and race relations. This situation also can exist when it comes to experiences with gender, religion, or politics, among other concerns.

The challenge in this type of interaction is that it can contribute to falsely perceived knowledge. Also, when living in cultures in which a class system exists or a culture in which majority culture and minority cultures do not share the same belief about similar experiences, various perceptive constructs of knowledge can cause divides and mistruths between different groups. An example of this is when various groups have strongly different beliefs about the same historical event. The result is that a strong belief about the other culture is felt (e.g., Black people are angry or hate White people, or White males are racist and sexist).

THE IMPACT OF PERCEPTIVE KNOWLEDGE

In a society in which a dominant culture and nondominant cultures exist, various levels of influences on knowledge are at play. At one level, the knowledge of nondominant cultures is centered on their cultural-historical lens as well as their having to adapt to the dominant culture's historical lens. The challenge here is that both dominant and nondominant cultures may have the same historical experience yet perceive the same historical experience very differently.

Take, for instance, the 1964 Civil Rights Act. Many in the Black community felt that equality was impossible mainly because of the historical inequality of wealth and economic opportunities in the community: at the time more than 50 percent of Blacks were in poverty compared to less than

20 percent of Whites. Therefore, some in the community felt more strongly about developing a community of equitable opportunities rather than equal opportunities.

The point of equitable opportunities was that the Black community would not necessarily be equal with White communities, but the Black community would be provided the same opportunities for success as White communities. There were those in the Black community who felt that actions like desegregated school busing were not the answer for bettering their neighborhoods. They felt that providing similar types of books, libraries, and school conditions as Whites had would give their children the same opportunities the White children had.

Children often share the view of history presented to them by their community (i.e., family, kin, church, etc.). These shared experiences lead to conscious and subconscious views, beliefs, and biases about relationships and interactions between and across various cultural groups. As this knowledge is embedded in memory, it becomes the framework by which individuals view interactions with one another.

Sometimes this knowledge still resides at the perceptive knowledge level. In other instances, this knowledge has been confirmed through some social interaction(s). An act can be negotiated from simply viewing an experience and merely connecting the observed experiences to some that appear relatable to that experience. Other socially negotiated experiences could confirm or put on pause this belief about interactions across cultural groups.

PERCEPTIVE DISCRIMINATION

What is tricky about making sense of complex cross-cultural interactions is how an individual believes that *ze* is perceived by others. As mentioned, as individuals make sense of information, the experience is typically negotiated and confirmed through interactions with those with whom the person has close cultural ties. Therefore, this experience may lend itself to some level of influence from that cultural lens.

Consequently, a person walking into a classroom or a counseling session with a counselor or the office of a boss from a different cultural background can have a subconscious perception that cultural bias is possible. If negotiated prior experiences manifest themselves into actions that closely relate to that individual's experience or belief regarding bias acts, this could create a perception of bias in the person's mind. Whether or not the other person intends to act in a way that is biased or discriminating, based on this person's frame of reference, the act can look and feel very discriminating or biased.

An example of this would be that of a large male of color walking on a campus. As he walks around and approaches others of different races, they respond to him by increasing the distance between him and them as they pass each other or females look at him cautiously as he passes them.[6] He then experiences others not looking at him when he speaks to them or not responding to him as he says hello. These socially negotiated acts can confirm his perception of this situation as discriminating and cause him to develop a mindset about this experience or similar experiences.

Whether the environment is indeed racist or not, the feeling of that individual is uncomfortable to the point that there is no other rationale, in his mind, that could help him understand why these acts occur. Sometimes perceptive discrimination is more subconscious than conscious. Let's take, for instance, the timeless study on stereotype threats. The study examined the academic outcomes of high-performance college students. Students were told that test scores would be based on race.

Based on the subconscious cue, students of color performed lower than Whites on the test. When race was not presented as a factor, scores did not vary significantly between the two groups. This study concluded that when college students of color faced negative stereotypes based primarily on race/ethnicity, this affected their academic performance. Therefore, the notion of stereotype threats is that an individual does not believe that *ze* can do something well based on some negative stereotype(s) generally made about that person's cultural or racial identity. This perception of discrimination can be more rooted in the person's subconscious than *hir* conscious frame of reference.

A prime example of this can be when a teacher points out that a student's family language is Spanish but lets the student know that Spanish is not to be spoken in the classroom. This directly or indirectly says to the child, "Your culture is not valued in the classroom." This leaves the child feeling inferior and may cause the child to hide *hir* difference from others so as to not feel unusual. However, all along, the child is left feeling the teacher and maybe even schooling as a whole is biased against *hir* family and their culture. Just as in stereotype threats, this can have a huge effect on the child's ability to perform well academically.

Finally, perceptive discrimination can also come from actual firsthand experience with discrimination, which may influence how one will view future experiences. These experiences can range from simple gestures associated with biases about the individual to a series of firsthand experiences that the individual has—for instance, any experience with a police officer of a different race in which the officer makes biased statements about the individual.

This can cause the individual to sense perceived discrimination toward both people of that race and toward police officers in general. Even if this person has positive experiences with people of that officer's race or other, more respectful police officers in the future, the individual would still have feelings of perceived discrimination. These feelings can be at the conscious or subconscious level.

PERCEPTIVE EXPECTATIONS

While an individual can have perceptive discrimination, those who are professionals can also have perceptive biases against or expectations of individuals racially, culturally, and in other ways different from them. The classic idea of females being unable to do mathematics or science as well as men comes to mind. Just as perceptive discrimination can come from things heard, things taught, or firsthand experiences that trigger biases, perceptive expectations can also manifest in the same way.

However, the difference between perceived discrimination and perceptive expectations is that when professionals hold a position of authority or act as caretakers or advisors, they can add to the stress of the individual whom they are serving. This is evident in the fact that schooling has been historically challenging for students of color. There are many systematic factors to point to why this has been the case. However, one of the constant factors is the lower level of expectations teachers have of the ability of students of color to succeed in the classroom.

EXPECTATION COMBINED WITH RACE AND ETHNICITY

It is challenging to conclude that expectation grows beyond what is experienced, viewed, or taught, especially when expectations of others are based on race. There are some who have a strong negative and disvaluing belief about others based on differences such as race, gender, sexual orientation, and the like. However, it is hard to conceive that the majority of individuals have such strong negative beliefs about one another. Yet what makes ethnic matching possible when motivating others to excel?

One theory is that individuals are unknowingly groomed to develop a belief or viewpoint about one another that is so embedded in their subconscious framework that they do not think but react to others based on mental triggers created over time. This can come from early or impactful experiences ingrained in the psyche based on preconditional views one may have about others and can become the frame of reference individuals use when interacting with others.

This occurrence can only happen through some systematic structure that has a significant impact on a person's way of thinking. Let's take for instance a systematic decision made in the 1930s. President Franklin D. Roosevelt enacted the New Deal to counteract the impacts of the Great Depression. As part of the "new deal," a home loan system helped families purchase homes.

This practice was the foundation for developing suburban communities. In this practice "redlining" disguised as "credit rationing" divided neighborhoods into green zones and red zones.[7,8] The green zones, mainly White communities, were seen as the most investable communities, and home loans were easily accessible to these families. The red zones, mainly communities of people of color, were seen as uninvestable, and getting home loans was challenging for these families.

As a result of this practice, Whites were better able to develop or continue a generation of wealth, while Blacks, only roughly two generations from slavery, continued a generation of poverty with no end in sight. In fact, during this time, over 75 percent of Blacks lived in poverty. Also because of redlining, green-zoned communities were, again, seen as more investable. Therefore, those communities witnessed better supermarkets, health care, and other opportunities.

Members of green-zoned communities saw their wealth increase by using their home assets as a liability. On the other hand, members of red-zoned communities witnessed higher interest on loans (if they could get loans at all), higher prices on food, and unstable rental communities. Also, families there experienced higher utility rates, given poor housing conditions and the lack of laws for protecting renters.

In the mid-1940s "Levittown" communities emerged, which doubled down on segregating communities by creating policies that excluded people of color from moving into these communities. The practice was supported by the Veterans Administration and the Federal Housing Administration both financially and in policy. While in the Southern states, Blacks and other communities of color were experiencing Jim Crow and hate-driven racial segregation, Levittowns, mainly East Coast communities, were building forms of racial segregation funded by the federal government. Today, there are more than fifty-three thousand homes in Levittown communities and more than 90 percent of their residents are White.

Later, *Brown v. Board of Education* and the Civil Rights Act were legal means to do away with inequitable practices of segregation. However, by the time laws were put in place to provide more equitable access for people of color, families did not have the financial ability to better their living conditions. As a result, the division between communities became a seemingly invisible line systematically based on race yet disguised to be based on poverty. Due to the historical system of racial segregation, this framework impacts communities and schools today.

As evidence, urban and semi-urban schools are more segregated today, with more students of color in schools where more than 75 percent of the population are other students of color, while White students are moving to suburban and private schools. These White students are continuing to have access to better opportunities for public schooling because in many states, property taxes fund schools. So families in communities with high taxes, based on the value of their homes, provide their local schools with more funding than do families in communities with lower property values. Further, many White families, given generational wealth, are better able to send their children to private schools.

As a result of this kind of historical, systemic series of events, it is understandable that people develop subconscious and at times unintentional mental frameworks about others based on the biases they unknowingly develop over time.[9] This viewpoint can cloud the way people perceive an experience involving others. As individuals flip such viewpoints to professionals engaged in interactions in which they are teaching, counseling, advising, or serving others whose race differs from theirs, their expectations of others may be preconditioned—that is, based on systematic experiences or thoughts that consciously or subconsciously drive their way of thinking of others.

These experiences help shape expectations, and the experiences may even confirm the individual's expectations of others. Laid out here are three ways these expectations can develop: (1) explicit expectations, (2) implicit expectations, or (3) situational expectations.

Explicit Expectations

A person's explicit expectations refer to the expectancy that everyone functions as that person sees or experiences the world or to the expectancy that popular norms are everyone's norms. This person also anticipates things functioning the way they do in the person's cultural framework, based on the notion that all subscribe to the same cultural experiences. These expectations come from a framework in which the person has little cultural experience with those different from *hir*.

Most (if not all) of the person's experiences tend to center around a particular cultural norm. This person assumes that everyone must have the same experience *ze* has, because everyone has a similar context. For instance, the person may say, "Everyone watches the TV show *Friends*," which is not true for many communities of color.

Implicit Expectations

Implicit expectations suggest that what is expected is based on or in comparison with dominant culture, and behaviors, beliefs, and actions are measured in comparison to a particular cultural group. In US schools there is an implicit expectation that "knowledge" is what the dominant culture perceives knowledge to be. Here, as a system, schools ignore the fact that conceptually, knowledge is relevant versus absolute and that knowledge is based on how one perceives information.

Perhaps knowledge must be factual and conceptually built on a set of principles. However, on whose set of principles should it be built, and do these principles represent a nonmonocultural perception of knowledge? Prime examples of implicit expectations are reflected in US schools teaching the imperial system of measurement over the metric system of measurement, selecting particular books as must-reads in the literacy curriculum, and teaching history within a dominant cultural context.

Situational Expectations

Situational expectations stem from the belief that the habits, behaviors, and actions of a cultural group are based on what has been observed about the group or how that group is believed to function. Given that dancing is a big part of Black and Latinx culture, it is often assumed that all members of these ethnic-cultural groups can dance. Likewise, all those of Asian descent are believed to be good at math. These expectations can also work in reverse and propose negative biases about groups.

These expectations are often driven by a combination of what people see secondhand (e.g., via the media) and their lack of firsthand experience with a cultural group. If one has never had a significant firsthand experience with a White man from a small town in a Republican state but has witnessed secondhand the behaviors of some in that group, one develops an expectation of that man or another person from that group based on that secondhand information.

Another way situational expectations can occur is by having an experience with a group and then transferring, or expecting that all experiences with that group will be the same. However, not taken into account is that a situation is simply that situation, and it may not reflect all situations with that group or similar groups. Note, for example, that there are various Black subgroups in the United States, from Cuban Africans to Louisiana Creoles to those of slave ancestry to new immigrant Africans. The same can hold true for Latinx or Spanish-speaking subgroups, Asians, Natives, and even Whites in the United States. These characteristics are merely visual—what is first seen of individuals.

Now throw in languages such as English, Spanish, American Indian languages, and then add dialects of languages such as Black-vernacular/ Ebonics, Spanglish, Chinglish, Konglish, Japanglish, and the like. Then consider the impact of regional influences on dialects; take for instance forms of US Spanglish like Chicano-English, Nuyorican, Cubonics, and others. This occurrence even exists on the global level.

Here it is easy to miscategorize a situation purely based on the first and maybe the only experience with or of a group. Sadly, a person's negative experience grows from situational expectations and the strong belief that all members of a cultural group share similar beliefs and behaviors. This results from *hir* relying more on a situational interpretation when anticipating a new encounter with a particular group of people. Again, if the interpretation is negative, a lack of tolerance of differences can be the result.

EXPECTATIONS AND ETHNIC MATCHING

So, going back to the question proposed: What does ethnic matching suggest? As people enter situations with perceptive biases or expectations and those perceptions lead to some level of conscious or subconscious stress or discomfort, the natural human reaction is to find a level of comfort or a sort of coping mechanism. Admittedly, in the United States individuals and groups may have deep historical racial conflict.

So, when ethnicity/race and the impact of race on knowledge and memory are at play, this takes on a whole new frame of reference that may be more deeply embedded in the subconscious. In this case, at some level racial/ethnic connection becomes that proxy that assists in coping with a situation in which an individual may feel consciously or subconsciously out of place.

On another level, ethnic matching may occur when a person feels motivated upon seeing a person of the same ethnicity in a position of control or power. This could lead to an individual feeling that the person interacted with is not judging the individual and has some level of understanding about the individual, or simply feeling more relaxed about interacting with the person of the same ethnicity/race. Nevertheless, these elements are still influenced by perceptive biases and/or expectations.

However, it cannot be mistaken that skin tone alone is the sole product of ethnic matching. There can also be other factors at play, such as skin tone combined with language. To an extent, these variations of experiences by particular groups in a society or community can affect how that group experience themselves in or outside that society or community. Take, for instance, the experiences of Blacks of slave-descent in the United States. The view of Blacks in the United States comes here from two conceptually different experiences, that is immigrant vs. nonimmigrant. Therefore, how these two groups respond to dominant culture play a role in how they are viewed in the United States.

What is more, the reason these Black groups enter or entered the United States can play a role in their perception of experiences in the country. Those who voluntarily come to the United States may choose, given their willingness to come to the United States, to adapt to the cultural structure of the dominant culture, as this may fit their reason for coming to the United States. On the other hand, those who found themselves in or came to the United States involuntarily (i.e., due to slavery, conquest of their land, colonization, refugee status) may not find the same sense of belonging or adaption to the United States for reasons that may be associated with choice.

The challenge here is how individuals overcome these cultural phenomena. When professionals engage with an ethnic group that differs from their own, how do they find a connection that is relevant? For a teacher, it may begin by presenting lessons, readings, and so forth that show authentic cultural familiarity with other ethnic groups. But how does one gain cultural familiarity that is not built on explicit, implicit, or situational expectations? One does so simply by engaging in authentic interactions with a diverse group of others. This is one of the valuable reasons for creating a diverse workforce in various areas and at various levels.

It is very complex for individuals, especially children, to create an intersection between perceptions, expectations, frame of reference, and knowledge. There is also a level of maturity and experience at play. Given these complex factors, it is understandable that individuals rely on external similarities (e.g., ethnic phenotype) in trusting information or making sense of situation(s). While this may seem like a primitive way of functioning, its effect may have more to do with individuals feeling safe, protected, or comfortable, or with their sense of survival.

TAKEAWAYS

The concept of ethnic matching is centered on the notion that people react or respond to that which is most familiar to them. Even consciously or subconsciously, individuals—especially individuals of color—are drawn to ethnicity often as that deciding factor. This is not to suggest that ethnicity/race is the only factor an individual considers when trying to make sense of a situation. However, research has indicated that it is a strong factor.

As mentioned earlier, expectations and perceptions play a valuable role when people of color interact with professionals of color and White professionals. Often this has to do with history, experiences, or other influences. Nevertheless, it is on the shoulders of the professional to work with others to look past ethnic matching and develop stronger levels of trust with students or other individuals they serve.

For best results, professionals should (1) understand their position of privilege and their expectations of their students, (2) not assume that students of color have the same experiences they had or should have had the same experiences they had growing up, (3) be open to other experiences and understand that all experiences are valuable, (4) not assume that they need to know everything about others' culture but be responsive to the cultures of others, and (5) work to understand culturally responsive practices that will assist in understanding how to create an environment that is responsive to the cultural experiences of those being served.

Based on what has been presented in this chapter, diversifying the educator workforce is essential to the success of students of color and to schooling as a whole. The field of education should determine which attributes held by successful teachers of color can be used in training teachers to successfully work with students of color. In short, evidence would suggest that teachers of color benefit all students, not just students of color. Still, the field must be aware that other fields are also competing for professionals of color, with less than 10 percent of college students of color choosing education as their major.

Most of these students go into fields such as business and social science. For instance, higher education is looking for more professionals of color because it has been shown that these professionals have been able to contribute to students of color having higher Grade Point Averages (GPAs), increased number of credits completed, and a higher retention rate by the end of these students' first year in college. Also, students tend to stay on campus to pursue graduate studies and complete teaching credentials at a higher rate than those not mentored by same-race mentors. The counseling field is also experiencing similar results.

Further, it is commonly argued that the reasons people of color are not going into teacher education is due to low teacher salaries, rigorous testing standards in schools, demanding licensing requirements, and the social perception of the profession. However, over the past two decades, the number of people of color going into teacher education has doubled in comparison to Whites. The challenge is keeping these professionals in the field, as teachers of color are nearly three times more likely to leave the profession than White teachers.

In response to the need for a more diverse educator workforce, initiatives such as Pathways2teaching, Oregon Teacher Pathways, Historically Black Colleges and Universities (HBCUs) teacher education programs, Teach Tomorrow in Oakland, and Call Me Mister have assisted in this effort. The purpose of these programs was in some cases to recruit students of color and train them to become teachers through high school pathway programs.

Also, some states have created initiatives to increase the numbers of teachers of color. In Florida, for example, the Florida Fund for Minority Teachers was adopted to recruit and train more teachers of color by offering a $4,000 annual scholarship to Black, Latinx, Asian, and Native candidates. However, not all states have invested in diversifying their teacher population. Through the new Every Student Succeed Act (ESSA), states are starting to examine their efforts in diversifying the field.

Chapter 3

Ethnic Matching in P–12 Education

One of the most effective ways to be a good teacher to any student is to build relationships. I truly believe that students will learn from teachers that they feel they can relate to and that they know cares about them. In my seven years of teaching I have tried to make this a priority in my classes. My classes usually have a high ratio of students of color, and I have tried to make connections and build relationships with these students. Of course, it is a bit easier for me because of my cultural background. I can relate with Hispanic students in my classes in terms of their home life, what their parents expect from them, and also the cultural expectation of academics. I would also say that my ability to communicate with them in Spanish helps them and their parents feel welcomed in my classroom.

—*Latino male teacher, Oregon*

This chapter discusses ethnic matching specifically related to teacher education. As mentioned, the term "ethnic matching" has not been heavily researched, but the concept has been historically researched, mainly by scholars of color, to express the impact professionals of color have on the population of students whom they serve. Most of this research has come from the field of education.[1,2,3]

Leaning on the notions of perceived knowledge and perceived expectations, scholars have historically shown a strong association between culture and knowledge. The rationale here is that there is a continuity/connection between the students' home culture and the teacher's understanding of how to link the students' home culture to the school's culture and instructional practices. Further, the thought is that similarities in culture can lead to teachers of color being better able to bridge the gap between the home and school cultures of these students.

Critical here is that bridging the gap between home culture and school culture supports the notion of cultural sustainability. Here teachers of color assist students in maintaining cultural beliefs, heritage, language, and dialect while at the same time engaging in the academic environment in a way the mirrors knowledge and learning to cultural knowledge and habits. Significant here is that knowledge, learning, motivation, and so forth are best understood when these elements are relatable. For many students of color, culture is that relatable construct.

On the other hand, White teachers may not see or understand the value of cultural sustainability or the threats to cultural sustainability for students of color. Note as an example the history of the death of many Native languages through the push to acculturate Native communities, done in an attempt to "develop" Native culture and assist Natives in becoming more "civilized," as a way to "improve" their social, cultural, and moral development.

Within this historical miseducation of the community, Natives strived to sustain their culture and language, while the US-based educational system was, and in many ways today still is, fighting against the sustainability of culture for many Native students, families, and communities. In an effort to acculturate Native and many diverse language communities, an early approach in US schools and communities was to kill languages that were not English by creating curricula and educational systems designed toward a more monolingual culture—even despite the push of the "forefathers" to make the United States a pluralistic country. For instance, laws such as the 1906 Nationality Act required immigrants to speak English in order to begin the process of becoming naturalized citizens, which was a way to use language as a mode of exclusion and discrimination. Even though the 1964 Civil Rights Act was the driver for bilingual education, the Bilingual Education Act did not take full effect until 1968, and not until 1974 in real terms. However, to this day, the United States does not have an official language.

More strikingly, in an effort to push out non-English languages, the United States only created language shifting into varieties or forms of English dialects rooted in the language of many Native or other mother languages. In early US history, the spread of the English language had impacts on the Louisiana French language, the Spanish Texan language, and US Native communities. This spread created sublinguistic forms in the Louisiana and Texas regions; however, the spread cause language death for most of the US Native communities.

But language death did not necessarily mean culture death. It did have a huge impact on culture, as language is essential to cultural identity. Even though many Native communities have spent decades restructuring their culture, a significant part of many Native cultures has been lost through language death. As nontraditional/dialectic English speakers battle for cultural sustainability through linguistic avenues, US systems still expect these communities to totally assimilate to standard US English.

As sublinguistic forms of English continue to emerge, linguistic assimilation is a much more complex issue than simply shifting from home language/ dialect to standard US English. The norms and structures of dialectic-diverse and language-diverse populations are a reflection of the linguistic norms and linguistic structures of their communities. Today Louisiana, for example, recognizes its strong Creole and Cajun linguistic communities and works to sustain these forms of cultural language and heritage.

Through its educational system, Louisiana attempts to assist in sustaining culture by making French a major part of the curriculum. However, the French taught in schools is Eurocentric, that is, from and of France, and the approach to the language does not involve the rich French dialect of the Creole—and in some cases, Cajun—communities and languages. Further, with more than 75 percent of the public schools employing White teachers to instruct populations of 50 percent students of color, the teachers are challenged to understand the relevance of cultural sustainability even though it is in the everyday lives of their students.

In the clash between students' attempt to sustain the value of home culture and the inability of teachers to recognize and understand the value of cultural sustainability in a learning community, there is a tendency for these teachers to consciously or subconsciously develop deficit or bias frameworks about students of color. Studies have found that White teachers are more likely to see students of color as having a hard time following directions, being immature, and coming from disorganized homes.

This view of students comes from a place of misinterpreting students' attitudes about school, as these students may possibly see no value in school as it pertains to their everyday lives and cultural practices. As such, students develop beliefs or have their beliefs confirmed that schooling is not relevant to the knowledge they've amassed and the lives they know. This, as mentioned in the previous chapter, can create social stress for some students and can leave them feeling confused.

Rather than recognizing the disconnect, teachers see these students' response to schooling and education as these students having a hard time following directions, being immature, and coming from disorganized homes. As these views grow, teachers' deficit thinking can bias their beliefs about the academic performance of students of color. Some studies have found that White teachers tend to rank the academic performance of students of color less favorably than they do students of their same race.

Teachers' deficit thinking often leads to these students being suspended, expelled, or placed in special education classes at a higher rate than their White counterparts.[4] However, when students of color attend schools with a larger proportion of teachers of color, they are suspended, expelled, or placed in special education classes less than when they attend schools with a smaller proportion of teachers of color.

The reality here is that the less time these students are in the classroom, the less time these students are engaged in a learning environment. The less these students are engaged in learning, the more these students are not gaining academic knowledge. This possibly increases the achievement gap between White students and students of color. It has also been found that when teachers and students' parents are of the same race, the teachers tend to have more empathy for the students' behavior.

Even on the preschool level, Black students are 3.6 times more likely to receive out-of-school suspensions.[5] At this level, a study found that White teachers have lower expectations of Black children, while Black teachers are firmer in their discipline of Black children.[6] As pointed out in the previous chapter, the study found that more of the teachers' biases were based on perceived expectations rather than actual witnessed behaviors of the children.

This trend also extends to higher education as students of color are more likely to experience problems of alienation, marginalization, and loneliness than White students are.[7] This may be because there are few other students of color to connect with or simply because the higher education community has such little expectation of students of color that it does little to embrace or welcome these students from a culturally responsive lens.

As imaginable, this can have a direct or indirect effect on the academic performance and social development of these students. Further, these students are often entering an environment that consists of monocultural curricula, cultural conflicts, institutional racism, lack of student support services, and even deficit expectations from professors. With this, students may be left isolated, with a loss of motivation, and as a result can be pushed out of school.

It is hard to understand why this systematic phenomenon occurs other than the fact that there are some perceived expectations that drive such interactions. They could have an impact on why the academic performance of these students of color is not greater. This is not to suggest that teachers of color do not have their own perceived expectations of students of color. However, it is hard to ignore that research has proven that there is something about the interaction between students of color and teachers of color that leads to these students tending to have a more positive academic experience.

Again, it is not the position of this book to say that by simply hiring teachers of color to work directly with students of color, the academic performance of these students will be resolved. In contrast, one can argue that there are a number of schools with high populations of teachers of color working with students of color, and these students do not perform at higher academic levels. Rather, the point is to understand why this connection plays a significant role in the academic experience of students of color.

In some instances, teachers of color can still be seen by students as part of the system of White rules and oppression, even when they share the same ethnicity as those students.[8] However, the ability to form a bond may be greater for these teachers. Still, one must ask if there are other systematic factors at play if we are to believe the research on the impact of teachers of color on the positive academic experience of students of color.

A factor to consider is that large groups of students of color reside in challenging communities with multiple risk factors. Given this perplexing circumstance, finding enough quality teachers can be a barrier facing schools in these communities. It can result in schools hiring teachers, even teachers of color, who are not quite qualified to work with students with multiple challenges outside of the school walls. In turn, the goal of enhancing student success can become a big hurdle in these schools.

The paragraph above is not to imply that teachers working in these challenging schools with a large population of students of color are not quality teachers. These schools are made up of probably the most hardworking teachers in the field. The point here is that there are not enough of these types of teachers working in the most challenging schools, which tend to be the schools with the most diverse student populations.

Another point to address is the ethnicity of the principal and the ethnic structure of other leaders in a given school.[9] It has been found that Black students performed well both academically and socially in schools led by Black principals. Today, 80 percent of public school principals are White, 10 percent are Black, and 7 percent are Latinx. One of the impacts of the low percentage of the latter two is the historical experiences of people of color in these roles.[10]

For example, right after *Brown v. the Board of Education*, roughly 90 percent of Black principals in integrated schools in Southern states were replaced, fired, or demoted. In communities today, principals have an indirect yet critical impact on the students' learning outcomes, those associated with all students, by establishing a strong academic culture. They also can set a tone that values diversity, equity, and inclusion. The field has now learned that when students of color interact with a principal of color, they are less likely to drop out of school than are students of color who do not have this same experience.

Although schools theoretically offer all children equitable educational opportunities, this does not happen without the intervention of strong leaders who strive to counter marginalizing forces. This requires educational leaders to engage in self-reflection, systematic analysis of schools, and confrontation of inequities regarding race, class, gender, language, ability, and/or sexual orientation. Once leaders take on this charge, they begin to challenge the status quo and work toward the social transformation of schooling that engages all students.

Further, when students of color see the majority—and in some cases, all—of their teachers and other school leaders as White, this can paint a picture of how these students perceive power and authority in society as a whole. In turn, this experience can shape the way these students feel about schooling, in cases subconsciously, and make them less motivated about being in school. On a psychological level, this experience can play a role in the value students may place on themselves in a school environment.

Nevertheless, evidence shows that teachers of color have positive impacts on the academic lives of students of color because of these teachers' positive thoughts and more favorable evaluation about these students. In turn, these students have a much richer learning experience. However, when moving policy makers to understand the positive impact teachers have on students, it is important to realize the policy makers are looking for more quantitatively measurable outcomes. Over the past ten years, research assessing the impact of teachers of color on students of color in terms of measurable outcomes has increased and has shown positive statistically significant findings.

IMPACTS OF ETHNIC MATCHING IN P–12

One of the most recent modern historical thoughts about the concept of ethnic matching or pairing of teachers and students by race came from the 1960 Colman Report. The data from the report showed that there was an increase in the academic scores of Black students when paired with a Black teacher. However, there was not enough consistency in the data to show that these findings were consistent for the general population of students. Nevertheless, even studies in the mid-'70s showed that Black students fared better in reading and mathematics when paired with Black teachers than when paired with White teachers.

The belief of many was that while the academic challenges of Black students were centered more on poor schooling conditions, as argued by the likes of W. E. B. Du Bois, Charles H. Houston, and the *Brown v. Board of Education* decision.[11] The belief was that Black students benefited more from Black teachers. This was centered on the principle that these teachers were better at engaging Black students, given the segregated nature of US culture. Many of these arguments did not resonate for Latinx, Native, or Asian students.

This lack of resonance may be contributed to the belief that the revision of the Indian Education Act or the revised Bilingual Act responded to the academic needs of these students. However, data would not support this assumption. Between the 1980s and 1990s and as schools started to become more diverse, the increasing need for a more diverse teacher population became more evident as teachers of color represented only 12 percent of US public school teachers. Therefore, this left many public schools with many White teachers who were less experienced in working with students from diverse populations.

As evidenced, studies showed that White teachers were less effective in raising the reading scores and vocabulary of Black students than their Black counterparts. There are two premises that can be drawn from these findings. One is that, given the familiarity with Black dialect, Black teachers are better able to interpret Black dialect and assist students in transitioning their dialect into "standard" English. This can be seen in some current reading curricula in Oakland area schools, in which teachers embrace Ebonics and assist students in translating and decoding this dialect to assist students in better understanding academic/standard English. A similar approach also appears in reading programs in some Native communities.

The other hypothesis is that White teachers may just be less experienced with these students and find it challenging to assist them, given the language/dialect barrier. Further, at the elementary school level, it has been proven that Black teachers are better able to increase the reading skills of Black students and Latinx teachers are able to increase the reading skills of Latinx students than White teachers for both groups.[12]

This has been shown at the kindergarten level and when Black students are paired with Black teachers from the beginning of kindergarten through the end of fifth grade. More significantly, Black students who had at least one Black teacher between kindergarten and fifth grade outperformed comparable Black students who did not have a Black teacher. These students' reading scores also increased more each year if they had at least one Black teacher, in comparison to scores for Black students who did not have a Black teacher.

More specifically, Black females scored higher in reading when paired with a Black teacher, while the effect was not the same for White females. Black females also scored higher in reading than Black males, even when both groups were paired with a Black teacher. Current research has paid particularly close attention to Black males in schools with increasing numbers of Black male role models.[13,14] In these conversations, it is important that Black females are not ignored.

The question here is why do Black girls benefit more, based on findings, from Black female teachers than Black males do from Black female teachers? Is it gender-specific, given that most Black teachers are female, or are there other factors at play? If it is a matter of these females having more exposure to Black female role models, then indeed it can be assumed that Black males,

Latinx males, and males of other groups will have that same impact on the academic experience of male students of color.

This is one of the critical arguments by scholars and professionals of color as a way to move policy in order to open the door for more male teachers of color. Especially addressed here are low salaries associated with the field, the stereotype of males not being nurturers on the primary level, and the stereotype of the lack of masculinity among male teachers of color. Another specific finding is that Black students who were on free lunch scored higher when paired with a Black teacher and did better in smaller classes when paired with teachers of their same race/ethnicity.[15]

Again, the positive role model effect and empathy for these students' living conditions have contributed to these outcomes. Simply put, Black and Latinx professionals tend to live in closer proximity to low-income communities than Whites do, even if both groups are from the middle class.[16] Black and Latinx teachers also are more likely to have contact or interact with families in poverty than are Whites. So, as these educators may live in different neighborhoods, cultural trends, including cultural language and dialect, may still be reflected in Black and Latinx teachers' lives.[17] Therefore, these teachers have a greater understanding of the cultural wealth that students of color bring with them to schools.

Again, results in reading may point to these teachers' ability to engage with these students through a commonality of language and other cultural experiences. The use of language and language styles (i.e., grammar and syntax, discourse style and interaction patterns, and behavioral norms) supports this interaction between teachers and students and serves as a tool for helping teachers connect with the students in their classrooms. The belief here is that even when being exposed to a teacher of color, this interaction could have an indirect effect on the achievement of students of color.

In essence, these teachers can offer the physical presence of a role model and well as be ambassadors of cultural values that may go unseen in textbooks and other academic materials and lessons.[18] In examining the impact of reading outcomes of Black students when paired with Black teachers, again, it is easy to suggest that language and/or ethnic dialect may influence reading outcomes associated with this type of student-teacher relationship. The same can hold true for Latinx students and students of various Asian communities.

This is one of the many reasons Natives hold language as a valuable part of their community and school curriculum. So a question left is, could these same effects be found in a non–language-related subject, such as mathematics? The argument here is that, first, it is easier to see the effects of a similar language and dialect shared by teacher and student on reading outcomes. Second, parents or guardians tend to contribute more to the early reading development of children, with less focus given to their children's early mathematics development.

Therefore, most of the mathematics skills developed by young children are mainly taught by teachers in schools. Unlike reading, where cultural language can be used to provide the meaning of words in context, the interpretation of mathematics constructs from a cultural lens may be a little more challenging than reading instruction. Similar to studies on reading, studies on mathematics show that achievement of students of color also increased when paired with either a Black or Latinx teacher.[19,20]

Similar math findings were discovered for Asian students when paired with an Asian teacher in grades 6 through 10. Even when examining math outcomes for secondary subjects like algebra and geometry; pairing teachers of color and students of color showed even greater results. The challenge for many elementary teachers of mathematics is in teaching students developmental and meaningful ways to learn and think about mathematics through a logical set of steps. Given the challenge of teaching mathematics at this level, teachers think of ways to include culturally related instruction.

Therefore, the application of these findings shows ethnic matching is relevant even when teachers are engaged with students in subject matter that is not directly focused on language and language usage. Beyond subject matter and the impacts of ethnic matching, there are other factors in the classroom and school in which teachers of color are valuable. For instance, in schools with larger populations of students of color, these students tend to do better academically when paired with a teacher of color.

This is not the case for students of color who attend schools with a low percentage of students of color. Additionally, students from socioeconomically disadvantaged schools that are often staffed with new or underqualified teachers tend to fare better when paired with a teacher of the same race/ethnicity. Even more critically, the academic scores of low-performing White, Black, and Latinx students were higher when ethnic matching was applied by the school.[21]

Probably one of the most critical findings in the research on ethnic matching is the amount of change or increase observed in the achievement scores of students of color when they are paired with a teacher of the student's same race. For instance, Black teachers account for 5 to 8 percent of the growth in mathematics scores and 16 to 17 percent of the change or growth in reading achievement scores. In comparison, White teachers only account for 2 to 3 percent of the growth in academic achievement of these students. Generally, when ethnic matching is not applied, teachers tend to account for roughly 6 percent of the change in achievement scores of all students.

RESPONSE TO DIVERSIFYING TEACHER EDUCATION

For years, it has been agreed that the US educational system is, for the most part, still conducting business based on a ninety-plus-year-old model, with sparse exceptions throughout the country. With schooling and its populations changing—especially with school choice becoming more popular—it is time again to answer, what is the purpose of public education? Also borrowing from the framework of Charles Wooden, what is the purpose of education for students of color?

Before diving into these questions, it is critical that historical errors in education serve as preventable measures, so they are not repeated as questions surrounding schooling today's learners are broached. The errors referred to here are associated with a schooling system that has not historically lent itself favorably to the overall academic success of communities of color. By learning from historical errors, educational systems must be attuned to responding to more diverse and inclusive populations of learners.

In avoiding historical errors, it is important to understand where the errors originated. An argument is that errors in education are based on the use of irrelevant strategies meant for Whites to educate students of color.[22] This is not to suggest that the content of what is taught in schools must necessarily change, but the way in which the content is taught must be responsive to the culturally, linguistically, and ethnically diverse learners in the classroom.

If educators continue to use strategies reflective of dominant cultures, students from diverse communities will constantly fall short of academic success. As talked about in the previous chapter, this way of thinking is based on a form of expectation about learning and knowledge that biases the way in which educators approach diverse populations. Intentional or not, this way of thinking can continue to represent a system that can be interpreted as historically, philosophically, economically, legally, and socially oppressive.

Due to this oppressive structure, students of color may continue to be dependent on an educational system that teaches from an educational/pedagogical baseline that stressed White superiority.[23] The problem with this system is that it could cause students of color to believe that their culture, social intelligence, and value were less meaningful than those of Whites, as well as create a sense of inferiority, dehumanization, and hopelessness that contribute to a lack of value and respect in schooling and all that represents education.

Scholars have given us evidence to combat these errors in the form of diversifying the educator workforce as a way to overcome historical mistakes associated with schooling. So, going back to the question of the purpose of schooling for today's learners and based on the current makeup of today's schools, the purpose of educating public school students must center on a way to make education engaging to all students, especially students of color.

Again, evidence has demonstrated that teachers of color can assist in engaging these students, and the attributes they bring to the table could be used to assist White teachers in better engaging students of color. As the findings in this chapter speak to the impact of ethnic matching, a critical question still remains: Are states adequately equipped in terms of having enough of an adult population to respond to the need to diversify their educator workforce?

When taking a closer look at states' populations, there is evidence for the need to hire more educators of color if we hold that these teachers can assist in enhancing the academic outcomes of students of color—especially given that within the next ten to fifteen years, students of color will be the public school majority. One way to assess the need is by looking at each state's ability to hire more diverse educators; do states have adequate numbers of diverse educators to hire from among their populations? This is a topic that will be further discussed chapter 6 on challenges in diversifying schools.

TAKEAWAY

The takeaway from this chapter is that teachers of color can have a great impact on the academic experiences of students of color in the school and classroom in both reading and mathematics. Yet there is still a limited percentage of teachers of color in public school settings, and the numbers of students of color in these schools are increasing at an alarming rate. However, this chapter is not suggesting that merely hiring teachers of color is the answer for educating students of color. It is agreeable that all teachers must first reflect quality.

Yet, this chapter proposes a great need for a diverse educator workforce to assist in combating the challenges that face public schools and that will continue to face public schools. This statement suggests that efforts by school districts to shape the workforce can lead to a system of diverse educators who are better equipped to engage with a more diverse public student population. Diversifying the field can also lend support to White teachers and leaders on ways to engage students and families of color.

Chapter 4

What Can We Learn from Ethnic Matching?

I teach because I truly believe that education is our greatest hope as a crumbling society. I am in love with learning. I recognize the flaws in the traditional education system, but I do not believe that our system is beyond saving. Through the ingenuity of educators and the resilience of our youth, education can be the saving grace of society. I'm passionate about equity and providing opportunities for young people to have a voice in their own education. We don't learn unless we participate in our learning. And that is why I teach.

—*Native Teacher from California*

The previous chapter presented the impact that teachers of color have on the academic success of students of color; this chapter explores what can be learned from this relationship. While the previous chapter demonstrated that teachers of color can have a significantly positive impact on the academic outcomes of students of color, it cannot be mistaken that all teachers of color are able to have this impact on students. As in any race of teachers, there are quality teachers and nonquality teachers.

Therefore, if the findings from the previous chapter on the impact of teachers of color is acceptable, it must be assumed that these teachers hold quality teacher characteristics. If these teachers did not, then the findings demonstrated in the previous chapter would not exist. As part of this book, several surveys and interviews were conducted with teachers and ex-teachers of color across the country to gauge the approaches these teachers adopt when interacting with students of color.

This tactic is based on the paradigm presented in the previous chapters that through ethnic matching or pairing students and teachers of color, the academic outcomes of these students would increase. These teachers work(ed) in both urban and rural schools with anywhere from 30 percent to more than 50 percent of the student body of color. The teachers were either African American/Black, Asian, Native American, Latinx, or Mixed Race. They taught in content areas ranging from science, mathematics, literacy/English, and elementary and early childhood education.

Surveys and interviews were conducted with only those teachers who could demonstrate that they were successful in working with students of color. Examples of these teachers' success include the following; One Latina teacher interviewed was from a rural community in which 50 percent of the students were Latinx. Her students' overall pass rates were 82 percent one year and 89 percent the following year. In comparison, the overall state pass rate was 67 percent. Another teacher, a mixed-heritage Asian teacher in an urban school where more than 50 percent of the teachers and students were people of color, taught students who had the highest percentage of growth in reading scores in the region.

Within a year's span, the school saw its reading scores among Latinx students go from 78 percent to 82 percent, meeting or exceeding expectations. This teacher also saw 92 percent of her students either meeting or exceeding expectations, compared to a rate of 46 percent for Latinx and 68 percent for White students at the state level. Other teachers' success was demonstrated by their elementary school's students going up two grade levels in reading each year over a three-year span.

One teacher who was interviewed taught high school math in an urban school district and was named the state's teacher of the year. Another teacher in a rural community was named teacher of the year and was invited by the Department of Education to work with the Ministry of Education of Palau, Micronesia. This chapter presents elements of teaching that these educators felt were critical for working with students of color.

Given that state standardized testing is not the only marker of success, teachers were asked what they did that was not captured by testing that demonstrated that their students of color were successful. One science teacher from a rural community explained that one of the things that she does that does not show up on a standardized test is making science accessible to her students. Given that scientific vocabulary can be difficult, she explained the key is in first building relationships with students and building a sense of trust.

When working with the complexity of scientific concepts, students can feel nervous at times because they do not know or understand these concepts. By building trust, these students are open to taking a chance at being right and at the same time feeling okay with being wrong. The teacher explained that she asks her students to challenge themselves academically, and because of the trust she builds with the students, they respond; they respect the fact that she has their best interests in mind. As such, she feels that her students work harder and are more productive.

LET'S START THE CONVERSATION

Let's start the conversation in this chapter by looking at the framework of pre-service teachers as they enter the field. As these soon-to-be teachers begin their coursework in education, they often enter with a strong kindheartedness for students they will be working with in the future. For instance, undergraduates in an introduction to an education course were asked what quality teaching is and how they would know quality teaching if they saw it in a classroom. These students used "good teachers" versus "bad teachers" as a proxy for quality teachers versus nonquality teachers.

"Good teachers" reflected those teachers who motivated the students to do well, who built a relationship with them, and who were positive. On the other hand, a "bad teacher" was one who was negative, lacked motivation, and who focused primarily on rote methods of teaching and learning. Interestingly, those students who had a positive experience in P–12 tended to have better grades and had better experiences throughout the program.

The challenge here is that most of those teachers who had a negative experience in P–12 tend to find their way to schools with high poverty or with high students of color populations. Often, many of these educators are not prepared to work with a challenging P–12 population. Why? It is because some schools with high poverty and students of color populations tend to hire teachers regardless of training level because there is a huge need in these communities with a small quality hiring pool. Sadly, some of those hired are teachers of color who had a difficult experience in school themselves.

Here this notion would seem to contrast with the findings on ethnic matching. Yet this is not the case, as will be described below. For instance, a factor that contributes to the impact of teachers of color is that the motivation of these teachers tends to come from a dissimilar place than White teachers. Simply, White teachers who go through a negative experience in P–12 and enter the profession tend to have a personal quest to right the wrongs done to them. For teachers of color, this experience can be more personal, yet these soon-to-be teachers see the greater impact negative teachers or schooling has on their entire community.

OK, back to the students in the introduction to education course. When asked why they wanted to be a teacher, overwhelmingly, the students said, "Because I love children." While loving children is a good attribute to have when deciding to become a teacher, what does this really mean? Does loving children mean that these candidates would transform their love for children into a love for that which each student brings to the classroom? As preservice teachers prepare for the field, is it reasonable for them to believe that simply loving children will make for better teachers?

This is not to bash teachers' love for the children in their classroom. Their intent here is understood and comes from a good place. However, by allowing this belief to mature suggests to preservice teachers that because they love children, students' success will come from the love they have for their students. While love can work as the centerpiece for teaching, "love" can only work if it can smother deficit discourse often brought to the classroom, rather than being used as conscious or subconscious approach used to make it okay to blame children of color and their parents, especially poor children of color, for problems these students face in schools, such as school-induced trauma.

Currently the situation seems to be that love for the children becomes the practice of subconsciously or consciously controlling and correcting students, especially students of color. It works as a proxy for "I make students' classroom experience challenging because I love them and I am preparing them for life." However, what is really being expressed by the expectation of a teacher with this mindset is that students of color lack discipline, structure, and understanding of success. So, through "love," these students will know better.

Yes, it is essential to love being a teacher and to love the children. However, this should not be the primary measure of a quality teacher. If this is the major framework in teacher education programs, then these programs are assisting in creating misunderstandings, conflicts, and disconnects between students of color and teachers as well as contributing to promoting racist mindsets. One of the ways in which these soon-to-be teachers can resist developing biased mindsets or deficit thinking is by focusing more on ways to connect with students, families, and their communities.

As touched upon in the previous chapter, teachers have to develop ways to connect the elements of learning in the classroom with culturally responsive teaching methods that engage students in learning. The approach of connecting with students can assist teachers in responding more effectively to the cultural components students bring to the classroom.[1,2] Further, this approach could help reduce mental and social stress and make the learning environment more relevant.

So, let's stop for a minute and assume that cultural continuity/connection is a critical approach needed by teachers to promote academic success. Let's assume that the connection between home culture and schooling would elevate the opportunity for learning for all students. Taking this approach suggests that teachers are equipped to move beyond deficit discourses.

This approach also suggests that the training of teachers would provide them with the tools to be more responsive to people of color as well as to

White minority groups like Roma, Lithuanians, and Polish, among others. This could, in turn, lead to teachers becoming more engaged with students at a culturally responsive level as a technique for blending the home culture of students with classroom content as a method of enhancing the academic outcome of P–12 students.

Therefore, continuing with the assumption presented above and the findings associated with ethnic matching, the sections below show how teachers of color connect with students of color through a culturally responsive lens and how this lens can enhance student learning outcomes. The point moving forward is to strive to determine which attributes held by successful teachers of color can be abstracted from their work and can assist in strengthening the approach of all teachers working with students of color.

With this in mind, those surveyed or interviewed were asked to explain the attributes they felt were helpful for teacher success when working with students of color. Before diving further into this conversation, it should be understood that attributes and pedagogy styles are two different approaches used in the field of education. Pedagogy deals with the philosophical view in which one sees learning happening in the classroom. On the other hand, attributes, in the context of this book, suggest essential qualities used by teachers to produce positive academic outcomes.

When asked to explain the attributes they felt were needed to be successful with students of color, the teachers suggested that teachers should have the following attributes: (1) The ability to build positive relationships with students and community, (2) self-reflection and honesty with oneself, (3) belief in culturally responsive lessons and student's behaviors, (4) empathy for the challenges students face, (5) patience and resilience, and (6) belief in one's students and willingness to advocate for justice. These attributes are known as the Attributes of Culturally Responsive Practice; below are examples of teachers showing how these attributes work in practice.

BUILD POSITIVE RELATIONSHIPS WITH STUDENTS AND COMMUNITY

One of the biggest challenges for White teachers when attempting to engage with students of color is finding a way to build meaningful and truly authentic relationships with these students even with the possibility of conflicting interest. One of the possible things that make this challenging is how teachers are taught to engage with students of color. The approach they are taught or develop on their own may be misleading from the start of their relationship with students of color. Let's take for instance the concept "culturally competent" versus "culturally responsive."

The word "competent" implies that a person can do something well, but not excellently. In education, competence suggests a student is in the high C to B range. So, competence would imply having about 75 to 85 percent knowledge of something. Therefore, to be culturally competent suggests that an individual knows a lot about another person's ethnicity/race, gender, or sexuality, among other attributes.

This is one of the possible ways that teachers are set up for failure. If one is from a particular ethnic/racial group, gender, or sexuality group, that person should strive to be culturally competent. Doing so would bring great self-identity, self-esteem, and great confidence to the individual. However, this could be challenging in itself. For instance, to ask a Black person to be 75 to 85 percent knowledgeable about being Black is a tall task, given that there are twenty-plus African/Black subgroups in the United States. This does not take into account the various African subgroups in the world. In the United States the complexity also stems from cultural differences in the South, Southeast, Southwest, Northwest, Northeast, and the Midwest, not to mention mountainous versus flat regions of the country.

Yet given commonalities of cultures, it is easy for that individual to gain a level of competence about various Black groups across the country. But without a historical or cultural framework to draw on, this would be a challenge for most people. Thus, it would also be a challenge to ask Whites to be culturally competent about people of color, as there are too many historical fragments and experiences to navigate.

On the other hand, to be "culturally responsive" implies that one is responding or reacting positively to the culture of others. This also suggests that one is not asked to understand everything about others' cultures. Cultural responsiveness simply implies that individuals react in a positive matter and use the cultures others bring to the table in a productive way.

A mischaracterization of this approach is in assuming that by not having to be competent about the culture of others, it is okay to function in a "color-blind" framework, which suggests ignoring all that is culturally valued or humanistic about others and only seeing the physical person. All people are the same; they are just wrapped in different skin. They represent layers of culture both physically and mentally that amount to a cultural framework that is of value. However, the point here is to embrace the cultural identity people bring to the table without stereotyping based on deficit or negative frameworks that might be associated with the culture(s) of the individual.

So it is conceivable that competing intersects occur when one party is acting in a culturally competent matter (i.e., asking a lot of questions about a person when the person does not even know the individual well, if at all) while the other party is acting responsively (i.e., developing a relationship with the individual by accepting what the individual brings to the table to share and having the patience to learn more while building a relationship).[3]

Again, it is key that people are culturally competent about their own ethnicity/race or culture, and culturally responsive as it relates to understanding others' culture. This is not suggesting that individuals do not make an effort to learn about the cultures of others, especially their students. However, it is critical that teachers understand that the knowledge they get from their students is interpreted through their own cultural lens and, until they dig deep to understand their students, they will always have culturally biased lenses.

As teachers take to heart the building of relationships with students, they will develop a strong and authentic way in which to assist these students to be successful in and outside of the classroom. Previously mentioned is that White and Black teachers come to the field with different motivations. When surveying teachers of color for this book, what was most striking is the value these teachers placed on connecting with their students and the civil responsibility they felt to the community. Even more importantly, these teachers believed in their students' ability to learn, to be successful, and to make a difference in their community.

One teacher explained,

A lot of the best practices that I learned concerning Students of Color were learned on the job. It goes back to relationship building as a main component of being an effective teacher with Students of Color. If you can do little things to build relationships such as pronouncing names correctly, being sensitive to the fact that they may be absent for a variety of reasons, and also trying not to over generalize the entire class and presume that every student has had the same life experiences.

Another way to look at this is through *humanizing pedagogy*, which consists of a method and practice of teaching that lessens the constraints between students, learning, and the classroom.[4] This approach is also less rudimentary while focusing more on a humanistic approach to schooling, learning, and education. In this approach, students are allowed to exist within a set of rules that leads to an environment that is culturally flexible.

An example of this comes from a former teacher who described an experience she had with a student from Brazil in her class. The concern of the school leaders was that the student was constantly late to this teacher's class by one to three minutes. The school leaders were concerned that this student had a disrespect for school rules and did not value getting to class on time.

The teacher then approached the student and found that the reason the student was slightly late to class was that other students were talking to her between classes. The student explained to the teacher that in her home culture, cutting a conversation short is a sign of rudeness. So she was being courteous by allowing her friends to finish their conversations before getting to class. The teacher then worked with the student on flexible ways to sustain her cultural values and at the same time work within school rules.

Building relationships with students, especially students in which social stress, cultural disconnect, and cultural sustainability are subconsciously or consciously perceived as threatening, is important. It is critical that the teacher is able to find a way to build some level of relationship with students as a way to engage students in learning and future academic success. For example, it is easy to reflect on situations in which a level of disrespect has occurred in an ongoing relationship, such as a working relationship, teacher/student relationship, or a relationship between roommates or neighbors.

When not resolved, these relationships can lead to stress on multiple levels. There arises a level of dreading the interaction on a daily basis. These types of relationships are impactful because everyone wants to feel valued or respected by others, especially if the relationship is an ongoing one. Then if the situation is such that the individual is dependent on the other person as a teacher, caretaker, boss, or another authority figure, the person in the inferior role strives to be valued or respected by the other person.

As cultural differences come into play, this adds a level of complexity to the situation, especially in a teacher/student relationship where the teacher wields great power over the student and acts as either a barrier or a gateway to learning. In this interaction, students want to feel cared for and respected mentally, emotionally, culturally, intellectually, and so on. With this, a grave responsibility is put on the teacher to create and keep the positive relationship with students.

As teachers show signs of building relationships, the teachers' ability to connect with students assist in shaping *hir* level of feeling humanized by their teachers. This is one of the valuable lessons that can be learned from teachers of color when working with students of color. Some teachers of color see themselves building relationships with students by engaging with the community. One teacher described the reason the community is a valuable part of the lives of students:

> I am respected in my community because of the ways I work to build trusting relationships with students and colleagues alike and understand our interconnectedness. My students', colleagues', and community's pain and joy are mine as well. Much of this is rooted in the fact that I was born, raised, and reside in the community I teach in. Therefore, I have much invested into things getting better. At the same time, the growing disparity and undeserved suffering that continues to target young people of color is still pervasive. My school site has the highest percentage of growth in reading scores in our region.

I'd argue that this is because my colleagues and I begin with centering community and what Abraham Maslow identifies as "esteem," and "love & belonging" human needs, as opposed to teaching to the test. Because of the sense of trust students have in us and the ways we center their well-being, I believe they are that much more likely to engage with rigor in the curriculum we present to them. In the words of Herbert Kohl, "Young people don't care what you know until they know that you care."

In essence, while building relationships with students, these teachers are fostering confidence in their students. Confidence comes from the teacher's ability to first humanize *hir* students, then *hir* is able to bridge the gap between home and school culture. Through this process, it is often misunderstood and assumed that by engaging in this type of culturally responsive practice, these teachers are not holding to academia's rigorous learning standards or high expectations.

This is not the case as one of the principles of culturally responsive practice is to expect a high level of academic success. In this, teachers set the tone for the academic and classroom expectations. Additionally, teachers expect that students will demonstrate the ability to communicate and present their work at a level that exceeds expectations. The challenge here is striking a balance between pushing students to reach a higher standard and pushing students beyond their potential. For many teachers of color, the feeling is that students of color are not pushed to high academic success.

The fear is that students of color on a systematic level are only expected to pass classes, tests, and other measurements at the level of "met expectations." This mindset is one that limits students of color and does not challenge these students to discover their true academic potential. In turn, this sets students up to not pursue college but to settle for a job-based rather than career-based life. Therefore, many teachers of color feel an obligation to push students of color to discover, understand, and reach their potential. What these teachers do not do is write a book or movie about this, because they are not shocked by these students' abilities and capabilities to learn.

One mixed-raced Latina teacher from inner-city Kansas City who was surveyed for this book explained that by connecting with her students and holding them to high standards in academics, they take responsibilities for themselves. She further explained she wants her students to learn and to become strong citizens in their community. Another, a Native teacher from a suburban school, explained,

I believe that I am successful working with Students of Color, though not in all of the ways that I would like to be. Academically, I drive Students of Color to achieve and perform at levels more comparable with their White counterparts than many other teachers in our school, district, county, and even state. Since the start of state testing two years ago, for example, my scholars of color achieve at levels comparable to their White counterparts, with only about a 6–8% disparity on average. While the gap is still there, it's smaller.

In terms of socio-emotional growth and support, I think I have good intentions but in practice, I do not always achieve the outcome I want. I strive to teach my scholars that until they're in a position to change the system (of oppression), they need to learn to navigate the system and be resilient in doing so in order to achieve personal success. I want them to understand that failure is not always their fault but that they can overcome it. In this, though I'm direct, I'm not always successful and so I continue to work toward developing this understanding in my scholars.

The teacher went on to explain that she pushes her "scholars" to take on leadership roles and be engaged in the community through internships, and she encourages them to be as successful as their White counterparts.

Above are examples of why teachers are willing to embrace the call of what it means to teach students of color using an asset discourse rather than a deficit discourse. White teachers may come into teacher education with a strong passion for working in communities of color, but they may need to shed their painful deficit perceptions and low expectations of people of color as a whole.

For instance, one teacher of color explained that the most important thing about teaching is in truly learning from the families of her students. This within itself requires a level of openness that forces teachers to step away from negative perceptions of students, families, and communities by accepting that they can learn from these groups. She further explained, "Many teachers I worked with were scared to go to people's houses or call their homes. I wasn't. I wanted my students to succeed, so anything I needed to do, I did. I've met plenty of parents/family members and they've taught me more about their child (or children) and about the community they live in."

The teacher went on to describe how she focuses on meeting students and families where they are and not where she expects them to be. She admitted that not all parents are "good" parents, but these parents also deserve to be heard, and it helps her understand the lives of the students better. She concludes, "The success I have had in my teaching, I attributed to my students' parents and community."

SELF-REFLECTION AND HONESTY WITH ONESELF

Read carefully here, as this section may appear to paint a deficit mindset of working with students of color. The reality is that many of the students of color in public schools are in urban and most times challenging communities.

But this is not the experience of all students of color. There are a number of students of color living and going to schools in suburban and affluent communities. While these students face similar experiences associated with being a student of color, they can also have different life experiences that impact their school experience.[5]

On the other hand, suburban and small urban communities are starting to have urbanlike characteristics. For instance, over the past ten-year span in such communities, students on free and reduced lunch increased to a percentage that was nearly triple that of inner-city schools. In addition, the suburban students of color population has gone from 19 percent in 1990 to 35 percent in 2012. These data do not correlate with the increase in free/reduced lunch and students of color in suburban schools. These data simply show the change in the demographic dynamics in these communities.

In association with this section, most of the teachers interviewed for this book related their experience with reflecting on how they interact with students of color in more inner-city communities. With this, these teachers were clear that resilience in working with students of color in urban communities was critical. These teachers spoke of not giving up on their students, weathering the storm when challenges occur, and taking on anger that is not necessarily directed at them. Sure, for a number of teachers, this can be a part of the everyday life of a teacher, especially in secondary classrooms.

However, a student of color who is trying to fit into a school environment or community where *ze* may be one of only a few students of color, or in a classroom in which social factors are threatening (i.e., Black Lives Matter; current issues of injustice, etc.), or who is simply feeling disconnected for reasons beyond the classroom or feeling pressure to be successful because of *hir* ethnicity/race can be facing challenges beyond those of White students.

Admittedly, there are many students of color who are in school communities in which there are dangers, community challenges, and other factors that can affect their emotions and ability to be attentive in the classroom on a day-to-day basis. Such a situation can drain a teacher's energy in the classroom or working elsewhere with students of color. As the teachers interviewed demonstrated, it is important for them to empathize with the challenges these students face and at the same time be able to overcome these challenges with these students.

So it is of value to the teacher to reflect on and resolve these experiences so as to continue to be effective. In some cases, teachers may start working with students from challenging communities because they want to have an impact on the world. A former teacher explained:

I started teaching because I wanted to save the world, but was really trying to save myself. At one point, the more I taught the more I became depressed.

I started having a hard time keeping relationships, and I had a hard time balancing my own emotions. This happened because I began to over empathize with my students. I began wearing their journey on my sleeves. I would feel their pain because at some point in my life, I once had their pain. There were times when I questioned my own character, actions, and motives in and outside of the classroom.

It wasn't until I was having a conversation with a student and started responding to everything the student was saying to me with examples from my own life, as a way of showing empathy, then the student replied, "It is not about you, it is about me." This hit me like a ton of bricks. I realized then that I had to deal with my baggage and I had to do a better job of reflecting on myself to gain introspection so I could focus on the needs of my students. I also learned that working in challenging environments could be emotionally draining and that I was human."

Like this teacher, many other teachers come into the profession with the mindset that they want to change the world by making a difference in the lives of students. There is nothing wrong with this motivation. However, if the motivation is self-driven as a way to heal oneself, then it is a discredit to students. This means that teaching is not about motivating students but about correcting one's life through the students in *hir* classroom.

This example is like a father wanting his son to play football at a higher level because the father could not and pushing the child for the wrong reasons. This action could cause emotional stress on his child and can affect their relationship in a way that is unrelated to the love the father actually has for his son. If the father does not correct himself, his relationship with his son can become dysfunctional. Like the father, the teacher's relationship with students can also become dysfunctional or ineffective, if the motivation of the teacher is centered on that teacher's own life disappointments.

On the other hand, if the teacher's motivation is to change the world through working with students who are experiencing hardships in school, the teacher must be real with *hirself* and not overempathize with students. This teacher's desire to change the world should be centered more on ways to assist students in gaining knowledge and then utilizing this knowledge as an instrument for making impacts in their communities.

Also, teachers working in challenging environments or in schools that are different in culture from their own have to be resilient and self-reflective. They have to deal with emotional difficulties that come with the job. It is easy to think about self-reflection from a standpoint of how to overcome mistakes in teaching or how to get better at instruction. However, one of the demanding parts of teaching is self-reflection on how to deal with situations that do not appear to have a direct impact on learning.

Finally, in the field of education, reflection is a valuable part of assessing if a lesson and curriculum are working effectively. Good teachers use this strategy to help them understand. They then collect and analyze information about everything that happened in the lesson as a way of improving the learning opportunities for students. Yet, *self*-reflection is a strategy in which a teacher actually reflects on self and how *ze* interacts with students in a learning situation. When working with students of color, the crucial part here is to take into account the cultural differences that may be relevant in an interaction at both the instructional level and in interactions unrelated to instruction.

A good strategy is to keep a self-reflection journal, a video journal, or an observation log as a way to analyze instructions or lessons and the way both parties interacted and responded to the situation. Critical here is that the teacher is able to take more responsibility or ownership of the situation as the authority figure in the classroom. This can be challenging for some teachers, especially if the teacher does not see the interaction as anything *ze* did wrong. Still, as the authority figure in the room, the teacher must find ways to connect and bridge gaps. With this, students, especially students of color, will feel a sense of value and respect and will see a teacher who is openly responsive to them on a humanistic level.

CULTURALLY RESPONSIVE LESSONS AND STUDENT BEHAVIORS

The 1974 US Supreme Court civil rights case, *Lau v. Nichols*, is probably the most valuable federal policy for pushing schools to be more culturally responsive. Some may argue that *Brown v. the Board of Education* was more valuable. *Brown v. Board* opened up the opportunity for students of color to access schools with White students. The case and policies associated with it did not push for or mandate that schools to modify their curriculum in order to make it responsive to a diverse student population. Yet one can argue that this is still one of the challenges of curriculum policies and practices today and reflects an anti-Black framework.

Another memorable policy is the Bilingual Education Act of 1968. This Act reflected awareness of the need for bilingual education, but it did not mandate school districts to participate in bilingual education. However, the *Lau v. Nichols* case was different. It was brought to life by a Chinese family living in San Francisco with children with limited English proficiency. The schools in the city felt they were providing Chinese students with equal education because the students had the same teachers, instruction, and materials as all other students.

The problem was that the students were not receiving equal instruction and materials from the teachers, because the students were not equally benefiting from the instruction in the same way as other students. The important point here is that "same" and "equal" were not interchangeable concepts. Teachers must acknowledge the differences that students bring to school, accept the possibility that students' background may have an impact on how they learn, and accept that "differences" call for making provisions that are critical for the educational development of these students. Again, "provisions" does not mean making the curriculum less rigorous.

One of the ways teachers engage with diversity in the classroom is through differentiated instruction, a way to develop lessons so as to anticipate and respond to learning needs of various students. However, when taught, this approach is usually centered on differentiation based on the intellectual abilities of the students and not on the influence culture has on learning.

An example of this is when a parent described his experience with a school in which their third grader had a project on US immigration. For this assignment, the students were asked to come to school dressed as an immigrant from Ellis Island. The question this father's son posed was, "Did immigrants only come through Ellis Island and what about slaves who immigrated to the United States?" So the father and his son spoke with the teacher, who pointed out to the family that this was an activity that had gone on in the school for ten years and "all the parents" loved the activity.

When the father approached the school's leadership with his son's concerns, he was told that he must follow the curriculum. Even as the concern was addressed with the dean of diversity, the family's point was "understood," but changes to the curriculum were not going to be made. So students of Asian descent were forced to ignore Angel Island, where millions of Asian immigrants who came into the United States were stationed between 1910 and 1940. This curriculum said nothing to the anti-immigration issues that resulted from the Chinese Exclusion Act, which was the first significant law that restricted immigration into the United States of an ethnic working group.

Also, the curriculum forced those students of Mexican descent to ignore border immigration, which mainly occurred between 1910 and 1930, when the United States actually welcomed Mexicans. During this time El Paso, Texas, served as an immigration station and the US Census showed that it contributed to one of the major increases in the Mexican population in the United States. Further, the curriculum dared not speak on the involuntary immigration of African immigrants between the 1600s and 1800s.

This teacher and school functioned in what was referred to as *explicit expectations*, in chapter 1. This approach suggests that it is the expectation of the individual for everyone to function the way in which the individual sees or experiences the world, or the expectancy that popular norms are everyone's norms. The school, teacher, and curriculum directly presented to their community of color that only White culture was valued in the classroom.

In this example, the teacher and the school ignored the values all students brought into the classroom. Yes, opening up the curriculum to be more inclusive would have led to challenging lessons on race and its history in the United States. Yet it is the country's history so why shouldn't all students know it, not just the students of color? This is one of those critical moments in which the student's home life and culture do not match the curriculum of the school.

Sometimes, when the interaction between the student's and teacher's experiences are different, the teacher must, in faith, take to heart that the challenges *hir* students face may be real even when they are not understood by the teacher. At times, the teacher may be able to use these students or their family's life experiences and challenges as teachable moments within the curriculum.

Further, as mentioned in previous chapters, beyond the curriculum and academic lessons, students of color are often targeted for behavioral problems at a significantly higher rate than White students. These students are suspended, expelled, or placed in special education classes less when they attend schools with a larger proportion of teachers of color than when they attend schools with a smaller proportion of teachers of color.

This suggests that the perception and experience of students of color when interacting with a teacher of color are notably different than the perception and experience of students of color when interacting with White teachers, with students of color having a more positive academic experience when having the opportunity to interact with teachers of color. The actions of White teachers might not stem from a conscious effort but from not having enough experience with students from different cultural backgrounds. Therefore, the White teachers may be anticipating that these students should act in a way that is more reflective of the teacher's cultural experience or expectations. There is a level of understanding or connecting with student's behaviors and interactions that is culturally driven for both the teacher and student. This was illustrated as a parent explained of the experience of his biracial sons when visiting his Black Southern family and his wife's White Northwestern family. He explained that in these two different worlds, his sons learn cultural differences that exist in the interactions, language, and conversations between adults and children.

When visiting his Black Southern family, the boys would explain to him that they found the experience formal yet informal. When interacting with adults, children are to be formal and have to use "yes, sir" and "yes, ma'am." They have to greet adults, especially older adults, and every elderly woman requires a hug. On the other hand, they mentioned that peer-to-peer interactions were informal, loud, and expressive. It involved lots of laughing and physical touches. When visiting their mother's White Northwestern family, they described the interaction as mostly formal. Conversations were rarely loud, there was little physical interaction, and some passive aggression was evident to them.

Most interesting was the boys' interpretation of their experience with their mother's family and how the children handled peer-to-peer conflicts with their father's family. The boys mentioned that in the father's family, peer conflicts are handled by peers, where sometimes there is an older peer there to help navigate the conflict. Very rarely does the conflict make it to the parents. But when they were with their mother's family, conflicts went straight to the adults.

This leaves one to wonder if these culturally groomed acts are transferable to adulthood, where White teachers may look to authority as the resolver of conflicts, as they witness conflicts or as conflicts are told to them by a student. When asking the parents about the differences in the two families' peer-to-peer interactions and if there was a notable difference in experience with teachers, the parents both said yes. Most noticeably was an experience their child had in a suburban school when he was in kindergarten and first grade. Their son had a White teacher in both kindergarten and first grade but a Black teacher in second grade.

The first two years, their son constantly had to go to the principal's office and had been threatened with suspension from school at least once in each of those first two years. During the year with a Black teacher, he never went to the principal's office. With the Black teacher, the parents were called in to have a conversation with the teacher once. The teacher-led conversation concluded with the teacher explaining the rules, expectations, and consequences.

What is most interesting, the parents explained that the Black teacher did not have as many rules as their son's other teachers. Also, the teacher expected the students to be able to handle problems face-to-face rather than bring every problem to *hir*. Also, the father explained that over time, their son had learned to interact in and navigate their two worlds. However, not many get to navigate two or more intimate cultural experiences. In turn, this limits teachers' ability to help students navigate and negotiate intercultural experiences.

Understanding the interaction of cultural groups can be critical in how teachers choose to interact with students and in understanding the perception of behaviors and interactions of students from diverse backgrounds. A Latina teacher from an urban school explained that she allows students to be themselves. She does not police their clothing or instruct them to lower their voices. She insists on not kicking students out of her class, even if they are angry or upset. She allows them the space to express their frustration.

She explained that she does not diminish their feelings; instead, she openly discusses them. As another teacher explained, "By doing my best to remind young people that I care about them—and that 'care' does not mean the absence of conflict—assists in my classroom management in the ways it decreases the likelihood of disengagement."

These examples are not to imply that these teachers do not have rules or boundaries. These teachers are simply taking a different approach to managing the classroom by building trust with their students through the acceptance of cultural behaviors. Again, this does not imply that rules are not present. But in the case where the teacher mentioned that she does not police loudness—and students of color can tend to be loud—loudness is seen as more about culture and a lot less about being disrespectful.

EMPATHY WITH THE CHALLENGES STUDENTS FACE

As mentioned in the previous chapter, the actions of White teachers in response to their expectations of students of color both behaviorally and academically might not stem from conscious effort but from not having enough experience with students from different racial, linguistic, or cultural backgrounds. Therefore, they may be anticipating that these students should act in a way that is more reflective of their own cultural experience or expectations.

The action of the perceptive negative behavior of these students can result from controlling and correcting the students as a way of loving them to success rather than having a level of empathy for them. It can be a challenge to empathize with others who respond and react to situations differently from how one would react in the same situation. Empathy within itself is a challenging behavior for many, especially when there is no cultural context or experience to help the person to empathize with others.

This is why many teachers of color may show more or less empathy for students of color in some situations than White teachers do. For instance, teachers of color tend to work in schools or neighborhoods similar to the school or neighborhood they grew up in because they tend to empathize with these student populations. As one Black male teacher from South Central Los Angeles expressed it, when asked why he wanted to teach in the neighborhood of his current school, he replied, " 'Cause I keep seein' me." Another teacher reflected on how her life experience helps her to empathize with students:

I am the middle child of seven in a large Latino family. I grew up listening to traditional family stories from my grandma, my first educational experience. My grandma would always say that in order to be fully educated, a person needed to have two types of education: education from home and an education from school. She would share stories about her troubled childhood, not being able to attend school due to family circumstances.

Even in her struggles, she managed to teach herself how to read and write. My grandma would always remind me that education was the most important essence of a person, and that no one could ever take it away. Without a doubt, my grandma was the first true influence towards my desire to become a teacher. Growing up in a small village in the state of Jalisco, Mexico and migrating to United States as a teenager were two of the biggest obstacles I have ever faced. School in Mexico was not an option; I needed to work to help my father support the family.

My neighbor, a retired teacher, Sra. Conchita, managed to teach me how to read, write, and perform basic arithmetic operations. "Efraín, jamás te des por vencido, ¡tú puedes!" (Efrain, never give up, you can do it!), she would say to me in her confident voice as I struggled to memorize my multiplication facts. I wanted to be able to understand my surroundings; to read road signs, advertisements in town, but most important, to be able to read books. She left imprints of letters, numbers, and new knowledge based on her life experiences.

My neighbor was a teacher by example and did not only teach me the basic skills of education but planted a seed in me of wanting to be like her, a teacher.

Moving to the United States was extremely challenging. I started sixth grade at the age of fifteen. I had to learn a new language, adapt to a new culture, and work extremely hard to catch up with my classmates. Because of social circumstances, I began to lose my culture, my language, and my identity. I learned that I had many labels in this country—Mexican, Latinx, Hispanic, and brown—which were viewed negatively.

I felt that my culture practices and identity were not wanted. Everything that had to do with Mexicans seemed to have a negative connotation. Therefore, I begin to step away from my cultural practices, and as a consequence, I was ashamed to call myself Mexican. However, I was not alone; I had caring teachers who guided me along the way. During my junior year in high school, I participated in a leadership institute for migrant students. It was there where I began to regain my identity and my culture. I was proud to speak my native language.

I fell in love with Chicano literature, and became a Mexican folklórico dance instructor and choreographer. I was proud to be Mexican again! I discovered a gift I did not know I had: the passion for sharing the Spanish language and Latino culture. I learned that we needed role models in our schools, Latino role models who were culturally sensitive and knowledgeable about our struggles. Role models who looked like us. My upbringings in Mexico and the many educational adversities I went through as a young adult, inspired me to become an educator.

Today, this teacher works with Latinx students, first-generation students, low-income, and underrepresented students who struggle to succeed in school. Here, she is able to empathize with these students through her firsthand experience. She shares her experiences and stories through a cultural lens to motivate her students to learn. She mentioned that this method gives her an opportunity to build relationships with her students and gain their trust.

However, it is important to note that empathy is not feeling sad for these students or in any way having a deficit mindset about these students. That is more on the line of sympathy, feeling compassion, sorrow, or pity for the hardships that students may encounter. Empathy implies that there is a level of understanding that can be pulled from a conversation, situation, or experience. Even if one empathizes with students, it does not suggest that one should give in to the students.

Some teachers of color may seem to underempathize with a situation related to students of color because the teacher may be familiar with a similar situation and see it as a situation in which students are very capable of handling themselves without teacher assistance. What makes having empathy important is that it is a typical response when the student feels challenged, misunderstood, or is uncomfortable with a situation. Here, even if the student's reaction to the situation is totally wrong, it is important to try to connect with the student to understand why the situation is uncomfortable. This is especially when the interaction is between a student of color and a White teacher with different cultural experiences.

An example here is when a Black father explained about his son being the only Black kid on his school's basketball team. At one practice, his son got upset because kids were calling him names. The child then responded by kicking a basketball against the wall in anger. The White coach's first response, with no understanding of the situation, was, "That is not basketball behavior," and he then told the student to take a seat. He later asked the student what his problem was. The student explained the situation.

After practice, the coach talked to the students about not calling others names. Then the students had after-practice shooting drills. However, the Black student did not feel satisfied with the coach's conversation with the other students, so he asked his father to come pick him up. When the father arrived to get the student, the coach told the parent that his child had a bad attitude because he kicked the basketball.

The father then asked if there were any other issues the coach had with his son to suggest that his son had a bad attitude. The coach said no. The father then tried to gain some level of empathy from the coach by asking if his son, being the only Black kid on the team, may have felt uncomfortable about others calling him names. The coach's immediate response was that he did not see color, that race had nothing to do with the name-calling, and that his job was to coach basketball and not be concerned with other issues.

As presented in previous chapters, this is an example of how some White teachers are more likely to see a student of color as displaying more of a negative behavior than the teacher would see in White students. In this situation, the coach was more concerned about the Black child kicking the basketball than the White students calling him names. Even after explaining to the White students that name-calling was wrong, his response to the father was still about the behavior associated with kicking the ball. The coach's lack of empathy for the student and his father made the coach lose the opportunity to connect with the family.

This led to both the student and father having a negative experience and the student feeling that he is not valued or protected by his teachers or coaches. For White teachers, who may not have the experience of having many students of color, the first thing is to try to put themselves into the student's position, and try to see things from the student's point of view. This may be difficult, but for that moment, assume that what the student is expressing is the truth. If the teacher can accept that possibly what the student was experiencing was the truth, the teacher would have a better chance of helping the student understand how to handle the situation.

The teacher should then try to validate that what the student is feeling is real. In the situation with the student kicking the basketball, if the coach took a moment to understand why this student was so upset about this situation, the coach might have helped this student feel more valued. Validating the student does not imply that the teacher is giving up or losing control of the situation. The key is to connect with students to better help them navigate their world and experiences with others.

Finally, rather than offering tons of suggestions to the student on how the teacher would handle the situation, it may work better to find out the student's goal in that situation and help the student find a workable solution. A point to remember is that in developing empathy with students, it is not about who is right or wrong but about connecting with the students so as to gain their trust and understand more about them as individuals.

BE PATIENT AND RESILIENT

In this section, *patience* suggests one's ability to accept or tolerate problems without becoming distressed. On the other hand, *resilience* suggests one's ability to recover from difficult situations. These are good traits for any teacher to have, especially patience. Resilience, on the other hand, requires a level of empathy and the ability of the teacher to rebound from a difficult situation with a student or with students.

Patient Teaching through a Culturally Responsive Lens

As teachers are now engaged in high-stakes testing, there is very little room left for them to step back, be patient, and keep up with the curriculum. Here lies one of the problems and challenges to both the teacher and students, as the approach sets up a system that encourages teachers either to misinterpret students' knowledge level or ability to learn or to judge students for their "inability" to keep up with the lesson. In either case, as the student struggles to make sense of what is happening in the classroom, the student can develop mental stress and a level of social stress, which can lead to students feeling frustrated, anxious, or lacking in confidence.

Further, it can be agreed upon that rote-based learning is anything but patient and culturally responsive. This approach also widens the disconnect between the lessons taught and students' home cultures. Teachers need to use patience as a part of their teaching strategies, especially when working in a culturally responsive environment or in a classroom with a diverse student population, in order to combat this challenge. A teacher has to have the patience to learn students' habits, behaviors, reactions, and cultural responses to a number of learning and social situations.

In this process, teachers must rely on their empathy skills in trying to understand why students from diverse backgrounds react or respond in ways that may be different from theirs. Patient teaching through a culturally responsive lens means first taking time to understand and get a sense of students' prior knowledge. It is much less effective if this is done by merely looking through students' files.

This approach is more effective by interacting with students to find out the way they think, how they solve problems, how they reflect on information, and how they demonstrate knowledge. Importantly, as covered in an earlier chapter, knowledge is relevant to the experience(s) people have. However, knowledge only suggests information a student might know. It does not suggest students' ability or inability to learn.

Additionally, learning and the processing of that which is learned are also relevant to the cultural experience(s) of students. This claim is not that cultural capital is related to a particular set of assets. Just the opposite: cultural capital, in this instance, centers on the rich cultural knowledge that individuals bring to a situation. This is why it is suggested here that knowledge is built on a person's ability to make sense or process information into meaning, not on what an individual already knows.

For instance, as neurologists have been able to demonstrate, there are two areas of the brain in which language is located for people who are bilingual. One location houses the person's native language and the other location houses the person's second language. Therefore, as individuals go to make sense of the information presented in their second language, the person must first mentally translate this information to *hir* native language before *ze* can fully make sense of the information presented to *hir*. As one becomes much more familiar with the second language, the processing or translation happens quicker as the brain gets used to this process.

It is not unreasonable to believe that a similar process occurs for those with a strong, culturally influenced English dialect. This belief is reflected in a study that took place a while back in which a group of researchers in a country in South America came across some street children selling items, and the researchers noted the children had seemingly incredible math skills. Fascinated by these boys' skills, the researchers wanted to explore these skills further in an attempt to help the boys adapt their skills to academic mathematics so as to steer these children toward a "better way of life."

When the researchers brought the boys into a classroom and tried to teach them mathematics using a standard curriculum, they failed to understand the process by which the boys learned their math skills. They simply disregarded the boys' skills, that is, how they processed counting and calculations. Therefore, regardless of the boys' number sense, the researchers with their unfamiliar methods were not successful in connecting with the boys. The basic point here is that the researchers were neither patient in their understanding of culturally based knowledge nor able to offer a curriculum centered on culturally responsive practice.

On the flip side:[6] a former Black college student explained how his statistics teacher helped him understand mathematics by connecting with the students through a cultural lens. The former student, let's call him Ray, grew up in a Southern Black community in which playing dominoes was a huge part of his culture. His family and community played dominoes at all family gatherings, birthday parties, cookouts, and the like. In almost every free moment, they played dominoes. As Ray entered college, he and friends from similar Southern Black communities would play dominoes for fun as a way to stay connected to their home culture.

Ray took an introduction to statistics course in his second year of college. Actually, Ray was not very strong in math as a whole. However, his college advisor thought that statistics was a different form of math and could help Ray complete his college math requirement. When he completed his first statistics class, at some level he could relate to the subject. Yet, he still struggled with the course.

His instructor saw that Ray had the aptitude for stats but was not quite making the connection with the subject. So the professor called Ray to his office one day. Their conversation started off with the professor just trying to get to know Ray. He asked about his family, what he was majoring in, and what he wanted to do after college. Then when the professor asked him what he did for fun, Ray mentioned that he enjoyed playing dominoes.

The professor then asked Ray to explain the game and the concept of the game. Ray explained that each player started with seven to nine dominoes and that there were seven suits of each number. The professor then asked him about his strategy when playing dominoes. Ray explained that he looks to see which suits he had the most so he could predict the possible number left of that same suit. He then explained that he would play to his strengths.

The professor responded to Ray that he was using probability, the likelihood of something happening and, in this case, the likelihood or chance that a particular domino could be played given a set of possibilities. The professor went on to help Ray understand stats by connecting class content to home culture using a culturally responsive framework. Ray went on to get his PhD and enjoys a career in which he is able to use statistics as a basis for his work.

As teachers work with diverse student populations, it is important that teachers develop the ability to be patient with their students and, again, learn how students respond, interact, gather, interpret, process, and demonstrate information. Students will learn nothing if the teacher is not able to connect them with information through an understanding—or at least empathetic—cultural lens.

RESILIENT TEACHING

Resilience becomes relevant as teachers engage with students, are faced with situations they need to overcome, and must find composure to be able to continue engaging with students in a professional or at times responsive manner. Two of the biggest challenges in the field are when teachers either overempathize with students or when they cannot empathize with students who are facing perplexing circumstances.

In either case, teachers must be able to work through emotions, situational stress, and other external stress factors so as to continue working with their students. One of the major reasons teachers leave the field is stress from dealing with challenging situations. The many students who are dealing with stressful lifestyles of their own, ones that impact their lives inside the classroom, need teachers who are resilient, able to bounce back.

Students will often present to their teachers the challenges of their life outside of the classroom. When they do, it is critical for teachers to not develop a deficit mindset toward the students or become overstressed about the situation; instead, they should be patient and empathetic as they work with students. However, the question now is, are many teachers built or trained to interact with students of different or challenging human conditions, to take on the onus of engaging with the students without taking on the students' stress, and to not become so overwhelmed that it impacts their lives in and out of the classroom?

It is challenging to understand where resilience comes from and what makes some people more resilient to stressful situations than others. Researcher Angela Duckworth suggests that it is "grit," the perseverance to reach long-term goals despite challenges, failures, adversity, or obstacles.[7] In relation to teachers, this suggests that if teachers' long-term goals are the success of their students despite challenges, the teachers must be resilient and have the ability to rebound from challenging circumstances with students in the classroom.

To clarify the use of the concept, "grit": here it simply means the teacher's ability to engage and overcome stressful moments in the classroom so as to continue focusing on the long-term success of the students. However, some educators have used grit to apply to students' inability to be successful in the classroom. For example, when asking a group of high school students about grit and what it meant to them, one male student of color said that he did not like the word. When asked why, he explained,

> In one of my math classes, every time the class did not do well on a test, our math teacher showed us Duckworth's video. It made me mad because it was not because I did not study hard or do my best. It was because I did not understand her instructions.

Further, it is imaginable that people could use the construct around grit to suggest that students of color do not have the characteristics or can learn the characteristics needed to be successful because they do not have grit. However, many students of color have grit by surviving the challenges of their day-to-day lives. To further explore grit, a sample of the teachers of color surveyed for this book were given the grit assessment.

It was found that on average, the teachers scored a 4.5 out of 5 on the grit scale, which suggests that these teachers are very gritty. Also surveyed were some former college and professional football players who, by looking at them, should not have been but were successful as all-conference and all-pro players. When asked why they felt they were successful, the common answer was, "I was afraid of failure." When reflecting on the interviews with the teachers for this book, they had a similar message; they felt obligated not to fail their students.

As described, one of the factors of grit is the longing to achieve something to the point that you cannot stop thinking about how to be successful in that arena. For teachers, this can be a good thing if the attitude does not consume one's life to the point of being unhealthy. If put in proper perspective, this attitude can lead to very successful teachers. It is possible to see how grit and resilience coincide. Both feature this notion of endurance and overcoming challenges.

Part of the drive to success must come from a level of commitment to the field. A group of two hundred preservice teachers were asked why they wanted to be a teacher, in an attempt to gain an understanding of the commitment of teachers to the profession and determine if there was something special about this group that made them want to teach. The survey used was adapted from the fields of music health and sports psychology, in which the commitment level of athletes was studied in order to try to reduce injuries.

In these fields, being overcommitted meant that athletes or musicians had a tendency to overwork their muscles to the point that they would become injured. In many cases, the researchers found that those musicians or athletes who saw themselves as serious or committed musicians or athletes spent most of their time engaged in their passion and tended to have more musical or sports-related injuries than others. The main reason was that they did not allow their bodies' time to rest.

The survey was modified and given to the teacher education majors. On a ten-point scale, the preservice teachers were basically asked how committed they were to becoming a teacher. What was found was that those students who were truly committed to teaching spent more time developing lesson plans, did volunteer work with young children, and were willing to teach all types of students regardless of demographics.

The commitment of these students toward teaching went far beyond that of students who were less committed to the profession. Further, these students had similar characteristics as the teachers of color interviewed in this book: a strong sense of grit and resilience, the ability to not give up, to keep trying, and to bounce back from challenges.

ADVOCATE FOR JUSTICE AND BELIEVE IN STUDENTS

Advocating for students is a tall order. It requires having a strong connection with the community and the issues surrounding the community.[8] For White teachers, it means looking at the world through the lens of their students. Teachers need to also be able to connect with real-world problems that their students face on a daily basis and be willing to check in with their students, especially around issues of injustice. Teachers must appreciate and embrace the culture of their students.

A teacher explained that it is a privilege to work with students of color. Because his students are grounded in a great love for their community, the teacher said, it forces him to be the best teacher he can be for these students. As he put it,

> As we know, children come to school excited to learn when they are in kindergarten. It is throughout their career that their love diminishes as they may fall further behind their peers or are criminalized because of their gender or race. Teachers must always remember that they are working with kids and all kids deserve that same amount of respect and effort one would expect someone to give their own child.

Furthermore, advocacy will sometimes require teachers to stand up for students even when it seems that it is the teacher and the students against the world. This does not mean having to be emotional, as young people will be. This is more about how the teacher is able to show students how to present a message that fights injustice. As a teacher, you have the best tool of all: knowledge. As witnessed by Florida students' fighting for stronger gun control after a mass shooting at their school, knowledge is power. Below you will find an example of how teachers are able to help students use knowledge to push policy reform and injustice.

Saraswati, a math teacher in Washington State, described how she helps students to make sense of mathematics in real life and understand how math can be used in an act of social justice. Additionally, she helps students understand how to use what they learn in the classroom to shape their world and how what is learned in the classroom can have a meaningful impact on their lives.

She described how she used mathematics and problem solving to resolve an inequitable yet real-life experience facing the students. She called this approach *critical consciousness*, which consists of student-driven projects that are based on their personal experience(s). An example from her math class is when she helped her students use concepts from her class to move school policy, which she shared at the *Seattle Times* Ignite Education Lab event.

The Seattle World School, where Saraswati worked, was moving to its third temporary location. In its thirty-year existence, the high immigrant- and refugee-populated school had never had a permanent location. The teacher saw the students' frustration and decided to work with the students to use mathematics as a way to demonstrate the impact this decision and previous decisions have had on the lives of students who attended the school.

In this process, the students used a trip planner software to calculate the average distance and time it would take them to get home from their existing school location in comparison to getting home from the new temporary school location. The students found that from their new school location, it would take on average three city buses and eighty-one minutes per day to get home, compared to on average two buses and forty-one minutes per day to get home from their current school location. The students, with help from their teacher, school, families, and community members, used their findings to convince the school board to move their school into a permanent reasonable location.

Often it is heard how challenging it is to include culturally responsive practice in math and science. Here, Saraswati presented how to use mathematics in an authentic, cultural, and responsive way. She continued to explain that as a high school math teacher, she believes that mathematics can be taught in a way that has her students investigating, forming opinions, critiquing, and challenging injustices and oppressive systems that are currently in place. This showed in the type of projects in which she engaged her students.

She also mentioned that students of color often get math education focused on them as rote memorization and basic skills that prepare them only for service jobs, which further keeps them marginalized and keeps them from going to college. Only introducing students of color to basic skills in any subject is deficit thinking that limits students of color. Yet this is reflective of Booker T. Washington's 1895 Atlanta Compromise Speech in which he implied that Blacks were to not overshoot their expectations.[9]

At the time he created a deficit mindset to support why Blacks could not achieve more than what he felt they understood: manual labor. The impact of this approach will be described in more detail later in this book. Today, there are many teachers and schools who continue to share this view about students of color. These students are often told that they do not have the ability to be successful in a four-year college and are encouraged to develop job skills while they are in high school and attend a technical college or a two-year college.

So they are encouraged to become civil service workers or to go into the armed forces. There is nothing wrong with these options. However, the educational system must move on from an 1895 way of thinking and assist these students in fulfilling their potential mainly because in the near future, a four-year college degree will be needed for all strong, career-based jobs.

The field needs more teachers like Saraswati, who set high expectations and expect that these expectations can be met. She shows a great example of looking at students' cultural backgrounds as strengths and making curriculum changes to incorporate student's lives. Saraswati went on to explain that when students of color are given access to critical thinking in mathematics, it is often culturally unresponsive and does little to connect the subject to the day-to-day lives of these students.

In her passion for mathematics education and her students, Saraswati spoke the language of reform, pushing for doing away with traditional schooling and mathematics education, and the maintaining of a traditional system of oppression and colonized thinking. She suggested that culturally responsive mathematics education is not the superficial addition of holidays or cultural situations within the context of mathematics through word problems. Culturally responsive mathematics educators look at a larger sociopolitical context and then design units and projects that are student-driven and based on forms of injustice that they personally experience.

On the elementary level, it can be understood that the teachers may think that this approach may be too much for this age group. However, these students are reading books with social justice themes. For example, the mother of a biracial eight-year-old asked her son the following question while he was reading a book on Jackie Robinson: "What are Jim Crow Laws?" After she explained the laws to him, he replied, "Oh, like laws that keep LGBTQ people from legalized marriage." He was able to use the expression "LGBTQ," a central topic in society today.

So it is important for teachers and educators to understand that social justice or the lack thereof is a significant part of the lives of people of color because it is a part of their history, and at times, everyday lives. This is not suggesting that teachers teach students of color to accept a life of injustice. The point here is that teachers of students of color give students the ability to overcome injustice and be active in eliminating actions of injustice. For people of color, injustice has no age.

TAKEAWAYS

The main takeaways from this chapter are that the teachers described found ways to connect with students outside of the curriculum. These teachers met students where they were and worked on connecting with students on both an individual and group level. For those in early childhood education, this approach is based on *developmentally appropriate practices*. However, this is only a small portion of the field.

These teachers described in this chapter hold the value of culturally responsive practices through basic principles of engaging with students on an individual level, connecting with students, being patient, dealing with challenges that face students outside of the classroom (i.e., those which call for resilience), and through engaging with student learning by ensuring that the curriculum and materials are reflective of the culture of students. These teachers advocated for students as they valued social justice and assisted students to use knowledge as a form of activism. Finally, these teachers were very self-reflective of themselves in practice and in their responsibility in students' learning.

Chapter 5

Practical Insight into the Impact of Teachers of Color on Students of Color

I believe that I am a successful teacher to students of color because I try to make sure that in my teaching that students still know that I care about them. I also bring in aspects of the history and current concerns of my students into my daily teaching. Overall test scores in my district are overall low and with new standards and new ways of testing learning, I don't believe that my test scores are indicative of whether I am a good teacher or not. However, I must say that I love that I feel like I witnessed a resurgence of a love for learning and school in some of my students who had begun to give up on learning. I built confidence by providing a safe space for student exploration and thoughts.

—*Black teacher who taught in Bronx, Boston, and San Bernardino, California*

The teachers of color surveyed for this book and experiences of other teachers of color outside of this book tend to show that these teachers view their students of color beyond academic content. Yet these teachers demand that the students display a level of excellence that shows that the students can use academic content outside of the classroom. These teachers' approach is purposeful, meaningful, and connects students' culture to the academic world in a way that moves curriculum beyond performance on a standardized test.

Therefore, one has to ask, beyond similar cultural experiences, what do teachers of color bring to the table when effectively working with students of color? One must ask mainly because not all that motivates people to engage with one another is based strictly on having cultural similarities. Thus, it is important to strive to determine other motivating factors that move these teachers to engage with these students. With this in mind, 150 former students of color were surveyed on their relationship between teachers and students of color based on some of the attributes described in the previous chapter.

The findings showed that 88 percent of the former students had a positive relationship with their teachers of color and only 65 percent said they had a positive relationship with their White teachers from kindergarten through twelfth grade. The former students mentioned that both groups of teachers built relationships with them, held them accountable, and disciplined them fairly. However, these students felt teachers of color did a better job of connecting the curriculum to their cultural backgrounds (90 percent felt teachers of color did versus 65 percent who felt that White teachers did).

The more diverse the learning experience, the better these former students felt about their experience with White teachers. Fifty-six percent of the former students who had only one Black teacher had a positive experience with White teachers. On the other hand, 80 percent of those who had at least four teachers of color had a positive experience with White teachers between kindergarten and twelfth grade.

These findings demonstrate two things. First, students of color who had a more diverse experience with teachers of color also felt more comfortable with white teachers. This makes for a more holistic educational experience. Second, students of color who had a positive experience in school felt that teachers of color did a much better job of connecting the curriculum to their cultural backgrounds.

INTENTIONAL APPROACH TO
TEACHING STUDENTS OF COLOR

Based on the initial information gathered from teachers of color for this book, these teachers collectively described their approach to working with students of color as teaching with a purpose and that their instructions, curriculum, and assignments were deliberately responsive to the everyday lives of their students. "Intentionality" is the best word to describe the approach of these teachers.

At first glance, the term "intentionality" in relation to the actions and work of these teachers seemed a bit problematic. The term did not explain the depth to which these teachers described their work with students of color. On one hand, the term is very ordinary and can be understood through the root word, "intention," which means to be deliberate or purposeful; it assumes that there is a level of independence involved. For example, people can be "intentional" in their actions so as to obtain a particular or desired outcome.

On the other hand, intentionality means something very different to phenomenologists and is at times a term that challenges the simple notion of independently acting for a desired outcome. Here, intentionality is a reference to the inseparable connectedness that individuals have with each other, whether they are aware of it or not, whether they like it or not, or even whether they do anything or not. This connectedness exists, and the connections are meaningful, again, whether individuals are aware of them.[2]

The term *in relationship* to these teachers' intentionality involves connectedness, relatedness, and inseparableness; it is a reference to the fact that individuals have a presence that matters and is connected to others' presence. It is to bring the casual use and the phenomenological use of intentionality into proximity, such that it pushes for the need to understand the degree to which teachers are aware of the connectedness and then act on this awareness.

Another view of intentionality is through the examination of effective practice centered on a phrase, "*critical social pedagogy*."[1,2] This pedagogy stems from a combination of critical pedagogy and social pedagogy. *Critical pedagogy* from educator/scholar Paulo Freire's framework is the teaching and practice that push back on oppression or injustice. For some, the construct may be hard to accept.[3] However, in working with students of color, in order to be effective, a teacher has to first admit that injustice and oppression are realities these students and families face.

This is not to suggest that injustice or oppression keeps these students from being successful but that these factors are real hurdles in getting to success. Social pedagogy is a framework centered on the notion that the function of teaching is a social responsibility that requires holistic education, which suggests that teachers should identify meaningful and purposeful educational practices by connecting practice to a social context that is rooted in culturally contextual experiences.

Therefore, critical social pedagogy is the practice of understanding and using social injustices of communities for the sake of learning and enhancing the learning of others within oppressed or marginalized communities. Simply put, education is nothing if it is not contextual. Therefore, an intentional approach to teaching from a critical social pedagogical framework implies that teachers must be purposeful and deliberate when engaging in the learning process within the cultural space students understand.

This does not mean "dumbing down" the curriculum. This may mean that teachers must learn more about the students' surroundings so as to truly impact their academic lives in the classroom. When working with students of color, this approach may suggest going a step further, which implies that teachers, as they plan lessons, curricula, and instruction, go beyond textbooks or their own frame of reference to make lessons meaningful. In this, intentionality also means looking at the growth in students beyond academics.

As students get a better grip on their social lives and the ability to handle their lives beyond the classroom, their lives in the classroom will also grow.

This begs the question, are teachers of color more deliberate or intentional in engaging the curriculum with the background of students of color in mind? For this purpose, the Cultural Responsiveness Intentionality Scale (CRIS) was developed to examine the intentionality of teachers through the depth in which they are aware of culturally responsive practice and the degree to which they are committed to intentionality in practice.

The notion here is that a teacher can be, on one end, unaware that any cultural connections or relationship exist and/or not care that they exist. On the other end, a teacher can be acutely aware of the connectedness, relatedness, and inseparability of their cultural presence and that of *hir* students and will act in ways that help continue developing the connectedness in, as suggested by Dr. Geneva Gay, positive, transformative, and emancipatory ways for all involved.

The CRIS was given to the 20 initial teachers of color interviewed for this book and then given to 180 randomly sampled teachers from various ethnic backgrounds, schools, communities, and grade levels taught. This survey assessed the levels of culturally responsive teaching where a teacher was viewed as being either an "oblivious," "irresponsible," "conscious," "activist," or "responsive" teacher.

While the CRIS data were from a nationally random-sampled group, these results are statistically liberal and should not be used to generalize the entire teaching population. However, these data are meant to provide some insight into the depth in which teachers are aware of culturally responsive practice and use culturally responsive practice.

Oblivious Teachers

The first category comprises a small percentage of teachers who are not aware of culturally responsive practice or multicultural education. These teachers are labeled *oblivious* teachers. The teachers who were categorized in the study as oblivious were from schools where less than 30 percent of the student and teacher population was of color. They mentioned that they were unaware of these terms because the concepts were either not taught in their teacher prep program, they were not really sure what the concepts meant, or they had not been trained to use these practices.

A small number of the teachers in this category explained that they felt multicultural education or culturally responsive practice did not matter in teaching or they simply did not care about culturally responsive teaching. In this, these teachers were oblivious to the cultural lives of students and others. They interacted with students through a lens that all was perfect. Further, the instruction and planning of these types of teachers might most likely have come from a culturally biased framework in which all students are equal and cultural responsiveness and differential instruction were irrelevant.

For instance, take the example given in the previous chapter on the lesson on immigration in which the teacher only wanted students to come to school dressed like immigrants who came through Ellis Island. The so-called oblivious teacher would function in a very similar matter. It would be a stretch for this type of teacher to see beyond *hir* frame of reference. The teacher would see no problem in requesting students of color to ignore their cultural background because this teacher would be more interested in the lesson and the activities planned and less on whether the lesson connected with students and their ability to grasp concepts that may seem not to be valuable to all students.

As mentioned in chapter 1, this method of teaching is what contributes to students' social and mental stress. In turn, the approach could force students to check out, and to develop a negative perception of the teacher. If this is one of several similar incidents the student has experienced, *ze* will begin developing negative perceptions of schooling altogether. If students' social and mental stress are not addressed, learning for these students will not happen.

Further, these teachers may also have "explicit expectations," which suggests that these teachers have had very little experience or interactions with other cultural groups. As described in chapter 1, this type of teacher expects that everyone functions the way the teacher sees or experiences the world and expects that popular norms are everyone's norms. Therefore, these teachers would teach from a frame of reference that things should function the way they function in *hir* cultural framework. Through this lens, if students are unable to adapt to this monocultural style of teaching, they will most likely fail.

Irresponsible Teachers

The *irresponsible* teacher is one who is aware that cultural diversity exists yet does not use culturally responsive teaching in the classroom. These teachers feel that they are not responsible for teaching through a culturally responsive lens. There are two types of teachers in this category. The first is teachers who do not use culturally responsive teaching because either there is no support by the district or they were not trained to do so. These teachers would like to use this approach in teaching and planning lessons with their students and community in mind, but they simply do not know how to do this work and do not seek to learn. Such teachers casually go about their daily teaching without giving much thought to culturally responsive practices.

The second type comprises of teachers who do not use culturally responsive teaching because either they do not think culturally responsive teaching
is important or they are not sure it matters. The thought here is that cultural
responsiveness is irrelevant in the classroom because pure instruction is not
biased.

Even though these types of teachers are aware of cultural differences, they
would prefer not to have diversity in their classroom; this includes diverse
learners or those students with special needs. These teachers would prefer
that cultural diversity be left to others who are more aware of "how to work
with" students from diverse backgrounds. Related to the lesson of immigration, this type of teacher more than likely would not have a lesson on immigration, to avoid talking about or dealing with controversy surrounding race,
class, or gender. This type of teacher would prefer to engage in lessons that
are centered on content.

If this teacher was to teach the lesson on immigration, the teacher would be
okay with the students dressing like immigrants from Ellis Island and simply
make excuses for why it is okay for all students to dress in this manner. These
teachers may even believe that culture is being covered because students are
able to witness various outfits from others. This belief may even be reflected
in the types of foods eaten during the lesson.

Another characteristic of teachers of this type is that they have a hard
time dealing with the very mention of race or cultural remarks in the classroom, the lesson materials, and/or text. As one high school student of color
explained, the class was to watch a movie that did not paint women of color
in a favorable way. The student asked the teacher if there would be a talk to
discuss the way the movie portrayed these women in a negative manner. So
rather than show the movie and have the discussion, the teacher decided not
to show the movie. Here, a very valuable cultural learning opportunity was
missed because the teacher was unable or unwilling to engage on a culturally
responsive level.

Finally, another belief of irresponsible teachers is that culturally responsive
teaching is covered through differential instruction. These teachers miss the
point; for them, differential instruction is the practice of providing different
students with different avenues to learning. The practice focuses on the cog-
nitive or learning ability of students and on meeting students where they are
from a learning perspective. What these teachers are missing is that just as
differential instruction is intentional in their teaching, culturally responsive
teaching is a practice that must also be intentional.

The remarkable thing here is that these teachers are aware that culturally responsive practices exist. Yet they refuse to use the approach in their
teaching. For some, to observe that they have taken courses in multicultural
education or culturally responsive practice yet still do not understand the

construct suggests that either the course was irrelevant to them at the time, the course was a mandated course with no true connection to the rest of their teacher preparation program, or they had a bias about cultural responsiveness before entering the course.

Conscious Teachers

The *conscious* teachers are aware of the cultural differences in the classroom and make efforts to include cultural elements in lessons and assignments. However, these teachers include culturally responsive elements based on a dominant cultural approach. These teachers are reflective of implicit expectations, as described in chapter 1. Here the teachers believe that what is expected is based on or in comparison to dominant culture and behaviors, beliefs, and actions are measured in comparison to a particular cultural group.

The CRIS shows that these teachers, while aware of culturally responsive teaching, did not consider the cultural background of their students with regard to lessons, assignments, or assessments. However, they felt that because they were open to cultural differences, they really took into account the cultural backgrounds of students in their classroom. For these teachers to actually open up to true culturally responsive teaching, they need to be more open to connecting other cultures to learning and implementing others' cultures from the lens of others.

These teachers may suffer from real interactions or engaging of cultural groups and believing that other cultural groups have value. Their approach may seem more of a missionary model in which they teach from the way they were raised rather than with an eye on the experiences of their students, especially those of students of color. The mindset here is that these teachers want to change or fix their students by having them assimilate into the dominant culture as a show of success.

These teachers may not see the error in this approach, as they may not feel that the approach is culturally biased in nature. These teachers may have been very attentive in their courses on multicultural education and really understood the basic framework of multicultural or culturally responsive practice. Yet they may have never had an opportunity to explore these practices in their program or clinical experiences.

Further, these teachers almost get what it means to be a culturally responsive teacher. They do attempt to be culturally responsive by trying to provide students lessons in which the points of others are included in the lessons. However, some critical points are missing. For starters, making a lesson inclusive is more than just adding diversity to the lesson, especially if the lesson is centered on a Eurocentric framework.

To be effective culturally responsive teachers, one has to focus on the intent of the lesson or the intent of what is to be learned. From a critical social pedagogy framework, this means that the teacher should focus the information being taught from a cultural contextual background on which the students' lives are centered. So if the intent is to enhance students' reading comprehension, then reading comprehension should be the intent. When students are provided with materials that are less relevant to their everyday lives, then more than reading comprehension is going on with the students.

There is a different level of thought that goes into understanding the entire context of the material. For instance, think about when you read instructions associated with something challenging like settings on a computer, a smartphone, other devices, or a car. Often this is not an easy task. Furthermore, understanding how to complete the task has absolutely nothing to do with your reading comprehension. It has more to do with the complexity of understanding a task that is not relevant to your day-to-day life, or what one may consider "common knowledge."

This also holds true for teaching from a culturally responsive framework. Common knowledge may be different as it relates to the experiences of students. As one Louisiana Creole mother who moved to the Midwest explained, her high school daughter had a persuasive-writing assignment and decided to write on women's rights. The student did not receive a favorable grade on the assignment, because the teacher felt the student used words and phrases that were not considered common knowledge for a sophomore in high school.

However, the mother explained that given her daughter's activist nature and being a woman of color in the South, what was common knowledge to her may not necessarily be common knowledge for others her age. In this example, the teacher should have cleared *hir* mind from deficit thinking of the student's knowledge base. By developing a more meaningful relationship with the student, the teacher could have come to understand why this concept was part of this student's common knowledge.

A question here, given the many responsibilities of teachers, is, how does one find the time to connect with the students to understand each student's cultural or contextual knowledge? The answer is simple: by asking questions either in person or getting other types of feedback from the student. This would give the teacher better insight into the students' knowledge base. In a culturally responsive framework, the teacher has to be willing to be both the teacher and the learner.

Activist Teachers

The *activist* teachers are fully aware of multicultural education and culturally responsive practice and use the concepts effectively in the classroom. These teachers will go to bat for their students—to a point. When there is heavy pushback from leadership or others who do not necessarily understand the impact that schooling, curriculum, and so forth have on students, these teachers will tend to back down.

Further, as mentioned in the previous chapter, teachers of color felt that an effective practice for working with students of color was to advocate for students of color. These teachers were the ones who taught from a culturally responsive lens unless there was pushback from students, parents, leaders, or the community. Then these teachers would be more likely to refrain from culturally responsive teaching practices.

These are the types of teachers who acknowledge their own biases as well as work to assist others who may be feeling marginalized. These teachers truly believe that biases happen and that culturally responsive practice is relevant in the classroom. Yet they will not initiate conversations about biases nor will they openly speak out against biases or racism. They will only respond to these actions if asked to address them and they will be careful not to offend others as they speak against biases.

Additionally, these types of teachers would do their best to learn about students' cultural and/or linguistic backgrounds. With this, they would plan activities around the students' cultural experiences; assess their assignments, tests, and lessons for biases; and make sure their materials and textbooks are free of biases.

It is easier for these types of teachers to work in an environment with others who are stronger vocally and who will speak up for students. If these teachers are pushed to defend their teaching or need to speak out on injustice, they may find it challenging for a number of reasons. These reasons include shyness, lack of confidence that they can speak truthfully for others or articulate their rationale well, distaste for conflict, or a simple fear of losing their job.

Going back to the immigration lesson mentioned above, activist teachers would fully engage in culturally responsive practice as a value and work with children and families to ensure that the curriculum was responsive to all students. Such teachers may even go as far as to invite people in to be a part of the experience and possibly have a guest come to the class to talk about immigrating to the United States. Yet once the teacher receives pushback from others, the teacher, while understanding the values of culturally responsive teaching, will back off of this practice and revert back to a place in which "everyone" feels safe.

However, the "safe" space is only truly responsive to a particular group and leaves other students, mainly students of color, continually feeling unsafe. Therefore, while these teachers' efforts to create a culturally responsive learning environment work on the surface, there is a level of intentionality that is missing from this approach.

Activist teachers are active in understanding how to connect the curriculum to the cultural backgrounds of students. They still lack the ability to understand the needs of students of color on a deeper level. As challenges and controversy hit, these teachers lack the ability to empathize with the challenges students face, be resilient, advocate for justice, and believe in their students.

Responsive Teachers

The *responsive* teachers are the ones who teach from a culturally responsive framework regardless of pushback from others. Interestingly, data from the CRIS showed that White teachers who taught in urban and suburban schools in which more than 30 percent of the faculty were teachers of color tended to be responsive teachers. This suggests that having a diverse workforce had an influence on the way White teachers responded to students of color. Further, these teachers implemented students' background in their teaching and advocated for students in their classroom.

Moreover, responsive teachers are those teachers who intentionally think about their students and the cultural background of their students in everything that they do or plan. Their mindset is on intensely motivating their students to learn. These teachers see their students beyond the classroom. They strive to understand how to connect with each of their students, how to bring learning to life, and how to use their students' cultural lens as a technology for promoting learning. In essence, they fulfill the basic needs of their students so learning can happen.

Related to the immigration lesson, these teachers would first develop an understanding of what their students know about immigration and what they know about their families' history in the United States. Then rather than just teaching about immigration on Ellis Island, the teacher would give lessons on Asians and Angel Island, Mexicans and border immigration, and the involuntary immigration of Africans. Then the teacher may explore other forms of immigration that impact the students in the classroom.

Finally, these teachers fight for fairness, inclusion, and social justice both inside and outside the classroom. Mainly because as they engage in the lives of their students and look beyond the classroom, these teachers see how practices, programs, and policies impact their students' ability to get an equitable educational experience. These teachers also strive to promote equity principles as a way to support the success of their students without backing down.

This approach does not suggest that these teachers are rude and tactless in their pursuit of justice. This is just the opposite. While these teachers have a passion for their work, they are also role models to students and work with their students with tactful approaches to dealing with challenges and social justice. More so than any other teacher, these teachers are intentional in their work with students of color.

This suggests that teachers who want to be responsive and intentional have to sacrifice habits, thoughts, and ways of engagement that may be more comfortable for themselves. In turn, they must be responsive, reflective, resilient, and have the ability to trust that the way students present themselves on a daily basis has value.

CULTURAL RESPONSE TO KNOWLEDGE

The intentionality displayed by teachers of color toward their students is for a purpose. This is not to imply that White teachers are not purposeful. It does imply that teachers of color are driven to see students of color succeed because they know what is at stake for these students as well as the lifelong challenges these students may face. Therefore, these teachers are driven, motivated, and deliberate in wanting to see these students succeed. Again, this is not all about the number of teachers of color but instead on their quality. Further, this does not imply that teachers of color are less driven and motivated to see all students succeed.

So what drives these teachers to engage students of color can be centered on the fact that learning outcomes have demonstrated that historically, schooling and learning under the US public system has been a challenge for these students. As a result, populations of color remain among the most impoverished groups in the United States, are less likely to be in a position to economically or politically move their communities, and are compounded by physical and mental stressors as a by-product of these factors.

Additionally, what is seen by these teachers both before becoming a teacher and while in the profession is lessons, curricula, and textbooks that are designed and centered on a White cultural framework, which makes it easier, even from a subconscious visual perspective, for White students to feel that the US educational system is designed for them. Yet students of color struggle to find their place both in US society and in schools.

Therefore, these teachers are self-saddled to help these students build the knowledge base to assist them in developing a life not driven by the dominant culture standards but by a standard that will transform these students' lives as well as their communities. The challenge of providing this help centers on learning and developing knowledge. Yet to understand this, it is important to reflect back on chapter 1's conversation on the types of expectations one has about learning, knowledge, or experiences in general.

As mentioned, expectations can cloud the way one perceives information. Again, given that White professionals make up more than 80 percent of the educational community leading the conversation on schooling and what is to be learned, they own what knowledge is and what is taught in schools. They may not understand that building a framework centered on their knowledge as the absolute knowledge to which all others must adapt makes for a challenging learning environment.

However, in a country whose foundation is pluralism, the framework does not connect with the history of the United States. For instance, John Quincy Adams was determined to make English the official language of the United States because he believed that if the United States did not have an official language, French would become the world language. However, he was voted down and reminded that one of the main reasons for independence from England was to have a more pluralistic society with freedom of religion, speech, and so forth. Therefore, to this day, the United States has no official language.

But the argument over the notion of absolute knowledge is not new. This is a debate dating back to the days of Plato and Aristotle, two philosophers who debated whether knowledge was absolute/true or relevant. Plato believed that everything was ever-changing and because of this absolute knowledge was needed to keep order. He suggested true knowledge is universal and political leaders and philosophy-kings should determine what knowledge was. This begs the question, who owns knowledge? Does knowledge only exist among an elite group or class of people?

On the other hand, Aristotle, a pupil of Plato, questioned how anyone could be certain of knowledge. He understood and agreed with Plato that there should be some universal principles around knowledge. Yet, he believed that all knowledge was fundamentally empirical. He felt that knowledge could be observed and categorized and was based on the relative interpretation of that being observed. Basically, knowledge is based on relative cultural background and experience of an individual. The question is, can both absolute and relative knowledge exist together? Let's go back to that five-year-old starting kindergarten.

As mentioned in chapter 1, the child comes into a classroom with a wealth of knowledge that is relative to *hir* cultural experience. Let's say, for instance, that this child is being assessed to examine *hir* ability to understand the concept "missing." Here the child is shown a picture of a plain house with smoke coming from the top of the house with no chimney. Then the child is asked, "What is missing from this picture?" The child replies, "There are no flowers and no trees in the yard." While the "correct answer" is that there is no chimney.

The child may have no experience with a chimney or simply the child looked at the picture through a cultural experience or lens. The absolute knowledge here is that the child understands the concept "missing." The relative knowledge is that the child saw the picture from a cultural or lived context.

Based on the framework of this book, that is, working with students of color, it is important to think about how one gets to knowledge. Again, as presented in chapter 2, the development of perceptive knowledge is the process by which an individual obtains working knowledge by taking what *ze* already knows and comparing it to what a new experience presents. The complexity is that the individual—student, in this case—brings in a frame of reference that is based on a cultural background that may come into conflict with the teacher's knowledge or presentation of knowledge.

To get a clearer collective understanding of the information presented in the classroom, teachers and educational systems must move to a framework that allows students' culturally lived experiences to be a part of the learning process, as mentioned multiple times in this chapter on connecting students' backgrounds to the curriculum. For students, knowledge is more valuable when it can be understood and expressed and shared with others.

If the US educational system continues to support and allow for biased educational practices, it, in turn, gives cultural bias power. As these biases manifest and grow, it will become more difficult to eliminate them, even to the point that those whom the biases are directed at believe the biases to be true. For students of color, this creates a self-fulfilling belief that they are not smart and cannot excel in the classroom.

Freire suggests that this phenomenon occurs because powerless groups often take on the views and beliefs of the dominant culture. This happens because of the magnitude of the voices of the dominant culture. Therefore, these nondominant groups tend to reserve themselves to a role of inferiority even in their own communities. Freire further suggests that for nondominant cultural groups to recover or get out of this dehumanizing state, they must revolt and create or push for a system that is more humanizing.

In a sense, this is what teachers of color do with students of color. In the framework of Patricia Hills-Collins's *Black Feminist Thought*, for nondominant groups to gain a sense of valued or feeling humanized, they must take ownership of themselves and how they are viewed by others. Again, for many teachers of color, their similar life experiences are part of what drives them to push students of color to succeed.

So often these teachers have seen through test score data and other educational measures that their communities are repeatedly seen as disorderly, wrong, or uncivilized. To eliminate these biases, these teachers strive to enhance the knowledge base of their students as a means of empowering their communities. For these communities to reach a level of empowerment, developing and expressing knowledge are what can help them change the paradigm, policies, and practices by which they and their community are viewed.

These teachers help change the paradigm by assisting students in changing their own consciousness in hopes that the knowledge their students gain will transform political and economic institutions so that social change is possible. Furthermore, by assisting these students, the concepts, paradigms, and epistemologies used to evaluate these students and their communities can consist of a conceptual lens that is collectively respected by the dominant culture. For this to happen, these students must see value in themselves. From this point, these students then can develop and evaluate themselves using their own concepts, paradigms, and epistemologies. However, again, this is only possible if the curriculum allows for their cultural experiences to be a part of the learning process.

TAKEAWAYS

It can be understood that when looking at their own critical social pedagogy, the relationship of educators of color with their students can be examined through one factor: common or similar experiences. However, it is hard to conclude that this is the sole factor. At a level, it seems that teachers are effective if they work hard enough to understand their students, or because they have a passion for learning and seeing others learn, these students will be successful.

Yet it seems that the findings presented over the past two chapters suggest the value of getting to know students, understanding their lives, advocating for them, and building a curriculum based on their cultural lives. These aspects may substitute for the common experiences teachers of color have with students of color, for the teachers have to have the drive, resilience, and endurance not to fail these students. In the view of the teachers of color interviewed for this book, failing these students essentially means failing themselves or failing their community.

If one was to stop and think about a teacher who was the most impactful on one's life, this teacher would hold a number of the attributes mentioned in this chapter. This is reflective of a teacher of color who talked about how one of his teachers had made an impact on his life. He mentioned that years later this teacher mentioned that she felt she really understood him, because, as he expressed it, "I reminded her of herself." His parent noticed that his son had a similar point of view:

> I don't get why my son loves the football player, Odell Beckham Jr. I wish he could find a player who was more in control of his emotions on the field. But my son sees it differently. He sees his strong passion for the game and understands the emotional drive that fuels Beckham. Why? I have to admit, for him, it is like looking in a mirror. I could fight him and hope to find a way to get him to find another favorite player, whom I think is a better role model.
>
> However, when I began to embrace what my son saw in Beckham, I have been better able to support him and help him channel his own passion. Now, I have been able to find ways to support him through who he is and what he brings to the table.

The example above is not to suggest that teachers do not have expectations for their students. It suggests that teachers find a connection and find possible similarities that can be used to move their students. Again, in thinking of the similarities teachers of color can use to move students, it is important to think about the ways teachers can connect with their students if they do not have experiences similar to those of the students they are working with. Even for White teachers who may not have cultural similarities with their students of color, a possible proxy for cultural similarities can be to connect with what students bring to the classroom.

As a former student of color explained about one of his White teachers:

> As I look back at my experience in school, I remember my fifth-grade teacher, Miss Carr. She was one of the few White teachers I had in elementary school. I remember being in a classroom with a number of students who, in the memory of a fifth-grader, were incredible artists. Miss Carr used this to her advantage many times. I remember one case in particular where there was an art contest with the local fire department. Students were asked to draw something to do with fire safety. Of course, I was nervous and I did not want to participate in the activity. This was also around the same time that my mother passed away, so my energy was also elsewhere.
>
> One day, Miss Carr pulled me aside and encouraged me to participate in the contest. So I did and every day that we worked on the project, there was always that bit of encouragement even though I never really felt that my work was anywhere at the level of the other students in the class. In the end, I got third place in the contest. While I never really drew anything since then, Miss Carr connected with me and encouraged me at probably the most critical time in my life. While she did not create an artist, she did develop my self-esteem and my ability to believe that anything is possible.

Learning and knowledge are nothing if they are not contextual. Teaching students to embrace learning is nothing if it is not aimed at connecting learning to experiences students can relate to.

Chapter 6

Challenges in Diversifying Teacher Education

Creating a More Culturally Responsive Educator Workforce

> You have to truly believe in the work you do, but also to learn to stand up for your students of color when adversities arise. Many people will never understand why their students are the main priority in teaching practice. Understanding diversity and privileges can be seen as something negative, but as educators, we must learn to advocate for our students of color. They continue to be the most disadvantaged students in our country, and we must use equitable practices in our schools and classrooms to help close the gap.
>
> —*Latina teacher from Oregon*

The previous chapters have shown how diversifying the field of education can equip schools to respond better to a more diverse US public school population. They have demonstrated that teachers of color are very successful in enhancing the academic outcomes of students of color, connecting with White students, and enhancing the knowledge of their White counterparts in working with students of color. Given these results, it is easy to argue that the most efficient way to increase the academic outcomes of students, especially students of color, is to simply hire more teachers of color.

However, this argument is more complicated than one might think. Multiple factors make it challenging to hire and retain a diverse teaching population. This statement is not suggesting that we should not strive to create a more diverse teaching profession. It merely indicates that the challenge to diversify the field of teacher education is a complex issue. This chapter presents the challenges associated with the ever-growing diverse student populations: recruiting, hiring, and retaining teachers of color; and the challenge in preparing culturally responsive teachers.

COMMUNITIES: STUDENTS OF COLOR POPULATIONS

The challenges related to today's schools center on the changes and makeup of US populations. Furthermore, when thinking about the changes in schools and students of color, attention is immediately drawn to urban school districts. While it is true that these schools often have the highest student of color populations, suburban school districts are becoming more diverse. Over the past twenty years, suburban communities have grown by twenty million people. More interestingly, in the twenty-five largest suburban communities in the United States, the percentage of the Latinx population is nearly equal to that of the Whites in those communities.

One example of these changes can be witnessed in the suburban districts north of Houston. Communities like Aldine, Klein, Humble, and Spring were once considered predominantly White school districts. Now Aldine and Klein student populations are reflective of many inner-city school districts. Spring and Humble schools are not far behind. Spring High School is now 40 percent Latinx and 30 percent Black. In a second example, the already diverse student populations in the St. Paul-Minneapolis Twin Cities area are becoming even more diverse, to the extent that districts in the area use the term "urban-like schools" to describe themselves.

Similar to suburban schools, small-town and rural communities are becoming more diverse, with a student of color population between 30 to 50 percent. Reports on rural education in the United States show that rural communities are growing at rates faster than nonrural communities.[1] The report demonstrated that just over 20 percent of students reside in rural schools. This includes fringe, distant, and remote communities, with three states with more than half of all of its student populations attending rural schools, and thirteen states with one-third of all of its students attending rural schools.

Additionally, students of color make up roughly 27 percent of the rural school population, with small percentages in states in New England and much larger percentages in states in the Southwest. When we talk about language diversity, nationally, 3.1 percent of rural students are English-language learners. Eighteen states have rural English-language learners with rates greater than the national average for rural English-language learners. Apart from Texas, North Carolina, South Carolina, and Arkansas, many of these states are in the West and Southwest.

However, Plains states such as Wyoming, South Dakota, and Montana are starting to see higher populations of rural second-language learners. Often mobility is associated with these populations, as many are migrant workers. Nationally, about 11 percent of rural students of color transfer schools in the academic year and twelve of the top thirteen states with the highest transfer rates are west of the Mississippi River.

This adds an additional challenge to schools. Here, teachers are challenged with constantly assessing and reassessing students' knowledge level. These rural teachers are also challenged with limited training in working with English-language learners, thereby creating a level of complexity to the classroom. Most times, these rural schools are limited in resources to engage this population as well. However, as this trend continues, many of these schools may have to rely on the business of those who are benefiting from this workforce to assist in supporting their schools.

Further, all US public schools, regardless of settings, are becoming more and more diverse and, in some cases, more segregated. Now, 15 percent of Black and 14 percent of Latinx students attend schools where Whites make up less than 1 percent of the student population. This, in turn, creates a new form of school segregation in which White students have left urban public schools or public schools altogether. As mentioned earlier, many of our largest urban school districts are less than 25 percent White.

This exodus has created or re-created a new face for US public schools. A critical point for schools to understand is that when students of color move to their districts in large numbers, it is important to comprehend that these students are from families with diverse cultural experiences. Further, as these students migrate into predominantly White school districts, they still bring with them a cultural lens.

It can understandably be challenging for school districts to become more diverse, but it will be more challenging for schools to expect these students to simply assimilate. For instance, Blacks, while gaining a sufficient level of wealth to move to a more affluent community, still live in close proximity to Black communities. Simply put, they interact with family members and friends from their old community and tend to go to church in their old community or similar communities at a higher rate than Whites do.

With this, the children of these families are also interacting with diverse cultures that may be different from the culture in which they live. So, as parents may gain upward financial mobility, other cultural trends, including cultural language and dialect, may still be present in these students' lives.

In this transformation of schools, many districts, regardless of community type, are being challenged to respond to an ever-changing school population. However, rather than supporting proposed policies to have voucher monies follow students to private schools or creating more charter schools, it seems a greater solution would be transformative reform directed at revisualizing public schools around more relevant curriculums, training, and school infrastructures.

A MISSING CONVERSATION

When speaking of students or communities of color, the conversation frequently fails to extend this conversation beyond the traditional framework. This implies that traditional dialogue around students of color and their place in schools often centers on students of Black or Latinx descent. Ignored are the challenges of students of color from other ethnic and/or racial populations. Even further ignored are the subcultural groups in the United States (e.g., Jamaican, various African immigrants, etc.). There is a multidimensional aspect to culture and ethnic culture that makes this work complex. Culture refers to a set of characteristic(s) that makes up a group of people. A person can belong to a culture of married people, a culture of parenthood, and/or a culture of religion. On the other hand, ethnic-culture refers to a race or common ancestry, history, and possibly language that influences one's cultural actions, attitudes, or beliefs. For instance, a person of US Black culture may be influenced by the historical style of music listened to by Black people in historical Black communities, otherwise referred to as "Black music." Unlike Rachel Dolezal, ethnic-culture is not something one can jump in and out of at will. On the contrary, people can change their cultural identity. For instance, one can go from marriage culture to divorce culture, and back again.

As the United States sees itself becoming more diverse, a critical population that is often not considered is the growing Asian population. When it is considered, it is thought of as an aggregate group. Yet, as explained in a previous chapter, there are various subcultures of Asians in the United States. Also as explained earlier, when looking at the academic outcomes of this population, our attention tends to focus on the success of the group as an aggregate. Often ignored is the fact that there are subgroups of Asians in the United States who are challenged academically.

Again, as John Ogbu frames it, groups are successful or unsuccessful based on how they are perceived by the dominant culture of their particular society or community. In both cases, the Asian student population and the Asian population as a whole are saddled with deficit discourse. Dr. Edward Curammeng once described in a conversation how deficit discourse could have an impact on Asians and Asian subgroups in the United States. So, for the sake of authenticity, he was asked to write a piece for this book on how a deficit framework impacts Asian students. Curammeng wrote:

> Asian Americans and Education: Section on Filipino Americans in Education
>   Deficit frameworks are harmful to Asian American students and communities because they reinforce dangerous and racist tropes rooted in histories of colonialism, imperialism, and White supremacy. It must also be understood, as a racial category, "Asian American" is comprised of close to fifty ethnic sub-groups.

In the context of education, for some, "Asian" and "Asian American" are not synonymous, whereas the latter emerges from a political context and is taken up as a coalitional and identity marker, the former typically references Asian international students.

This distinction is significant as some institutional data collection practices inflate numbers and ultimately reinforce notions that as a whole, Asian Americans fare well in schools and academics. Because of tendencies to uncritically collapse all of these ethnic subgroups under the category of "Asian American," the unique needs of each group remain hidden. Said differently, nuance found within the histories, experiences, and sociocultural contexts of various populations within Asian America must be engaged to ascertain best practices and supports for students, families, and communities.

In the case of Filipino Americans, their relationship to education has long been shaped by vexed relationships with colonialism. From this perspective, education scholars focused on Filipino Americans have found, for example, their "invisibility" in history textbooks and sparse culturally relevant curricula; challenges with access to postsecondary education; and a lack of Filipino American professors. In my own work with teachers of color, I have found ethnic studies and Asian American studies as important and critical interventions needed in education research and practice.

Ethnic studies provides tools, critical frameworks, and pedagogies to precisely interrogate systems of power and challenge structures that rest upon deficit frames salient in schooling. In sum, ethnic and Asian American studies are productive sites for advancing social and racial justice for students and teachers of color.

Proposed here is that as schools become more diverse, educators must not be in a hurry to dichotomously categorize others as a way of comparing them to dominant cultural groups. As with many ethnic groups that are measured by their category—the larger regional group—each subgroup has within it its own subcultures and mininarratives, forming the subgroup's culture.

There are also a number of other major biases placed on Asian culture and sold as the mainframe of Asian communities; they especially center on gender-biased views that present Asian men as doormats and Asian women as casual sex partners. Such views place a level of dehumanizing characteristics on these groups. Additionally, Asians make up perhaps one of the most underrepresented, misrepresented, and stereotyped ethnic groups in the media and in US culture.

This representation has had direct and indirect impacts on this group in schools. For instance, US Asian students are frequently perceived as academic overachievers, nerds who lack appropriate social skills and communication skills compared to other ethnic groups. The challenge here is that this population is becoming a large part of the US community; just as there are various subgroups of Latinx, Natives, people of African descent, and even those of European descent, Asian populations fit this same mold.

TEACHERS OF COLOR

The field has widely accepted that one of the reasons for the shortage of teachers of color is that people of color are simply not selecting education as a career.[2] However, data from the Schools and Staffing Survey and the Teacher Follow-up Survey showed that over a span of two decades, the percentage of teachers of color grew 96 percent in comparison to 41 percent of White teachers during that time.[3]

The increase can be contributed to the concentrated efforts by Historical Black Colleges and Universities (HBCU) teacher education programs; special programs such as Call Me Mister; the North Carolina Teaching Fellows Scholarship Program; and alternative programs such as Teach for America, the New Teacher Project-Fellowship Program, the Urban Teacher Enhancement Program, and Teach Tomorrow in Oakland. These programs have deliberately focused on producing teachers of color.

HBCUs alone generate half of the nation's Black teachers. Alternative programs produce roughly 25 percent of the total of Black and Latinx teachers compared to 11 percent of the total White teacher workforce.[4] This within itself suggests an interesting challenge, as will be shown later in this chapter. HBCUs, university-based programs, and scholarship programs are based on traditional preservice teacher education models in which students go through a sequential process of developing as teachers. These programs have proven to be very effective in enhancing the learning of students of color.

However, there are mixed reviews on whether alternative teacher education programs produce the same effects. What is known is that teachers of color tend to work in highly diverse schools, are primarily employed in public schools serving high-poverty and/or urban communities at a higher rate than their White counterparts.[5] These teachers are nearly three times more likely than White teachers to work in schools with students from families and communities with high stress factors. They are also more willing to engage with and stay in those in schools with a higher percentage of students who are not performing well academically than White teachers are.

This shows that these teachers are willing to take on a greater responsibility of working with students in the most challenging of circumstances. This also mirrors why these teachers are so invested in learning and how learning plays out in their community. Often the goal of preservice teachers is to work in school districts in affluent neighborhoods or school districts with low-risk factors. However, often teachers of color see teaching as more of a civic call to action and a way to better the lives of students and communities of color. Additionally, prior to the early 1980s, Blacks often sought teaching as a noble profession.

Now, with many help-profession fields looking to diversify their profession, we are seeing fewer Blacks and other communities of color looking to become educators. Now there are many other ways professionals of color can serve their communities, such as through the medical field, health professions, counseling, and the like. For those teachers of color who stay in the profession, many tend to leave or transfer from their original school at a higher rate than their White counterparts. In the late 1980s, there was a 0.7 percent difference in the turnover rate between teachers of color and White teachers.

In the following two decades there was a 3 to 4 percent difference in the turnover rate between teachers of color and White teachers. Reasons for leaving the profession include the lack of being able to make decisions, or the relative degree of individual instructional autonomy when working with students. These teachers have also been found to feel less satisfied with the way their school was run in comparison to White teachers. This issue indicates that there is a level of cultural disconnect between schooling and the philosophy of teaching by teachers of color.

Again, often when teachers of color enter the field, the approach is centered on impacting positive change in their communities and for culturally responsive reasons. It is understandable that these teachers may see that the curriculum and lessons do not have a culturally responsive lens; in an effort to communicate with others, including supervisors, about ideas to make educational practices more culturally relevant, these teachers can experience a conflict between their desire to change the way students are taught and the efforts of their supervisors to meet state assessment standards. This is a critical challenge as the demand on high-stakes standardized testing has all but taken away teachers' abilities to individualize the curriculum within their classrooms and across the same grade level.

THE OTHER SIDE OF TEACHERS OF COLOR

As this book explores the impact of teachers of color on the academic experiences of students of color, it would be in error not to talk about some of the challenges quality teachers of color face when working with teachers of color who approach teaching through a different lens. For instance, postslavery, there was a huge debate between Booker T. Washington and W. E. B. Du Bois on the purpose of education and economic progress for Blacks. This debate still shadows the way Blacks and other communities of color approach education today.

Washington focused on the educational purpose of Blacks much through a deficit framework in which he embraced that education should provide Blacks with the basic utensils for establishing a normal lifestyle that did not compete with the lifestyles of Whites or that would be a threat to Whites as the dominant culture. Within this framework, Blacks were to be taught basic skills centered on manual labor. This approach prompted many local school districts to create "manual" high schools in Black neighborhoods. Today, Manual High School in Denver still carries the name "Manual."

Based on Washington's thought about schooling for Blacks, the curriculum centered on basic reading and mathematics skills and primarily on discipline. This approach holds to the belief that students of color are less disciplined and organized and that they need to be taught these skills. This approach proposes that academics is not the framework for school and that learning to behave is the center of the curriculum. This approach includes punishment charts and other methods for controlling behaviors.

This methodology can be still seen in classrooms today as some teachers of color buy into the deficit mindset that students of color have behavioral challenges and schools should be centered on behavioral control. Yes, there is a level of classroom management and behavior control in teaching. But it should not be the major focus on teaching students, especially students of color. So, based on this framework, these teachers have a scripted approach to teaching in which basic skills for students of color are the main focus of the curriculum.

These teachers see the students as a challenge rather than an opportunity. The students' ability to learn is not first in the mind of these teachers. These teachers often teach students in the poorest schools and with students with the highest need. This is not to suggest that all of the teachers in these environments fit this mode. This statement implies that often, deficit-thinking teachers tend to teach in these environments with the belief that they are making an impact on the community through a tough-love framework.

Instead, what these educators are doing is creating an institution-like environment in which students grow accustomed to and learn to behave and perform within that environment. These students have no belief in themselves; thinking that they cannot learn, they buy into the fact that behaviors and not academic abilities are what is measured, and they see school only as a mandatory part of their lives.

Also, of the original fifty-two teachers of color interviewed for this book, only twenty could demonstrate that they were effective with working with students of color through testing, seeing the growth in students, increase in attendance, increase in attention in the classroom, or more class participation, among other measures. The thirty-two teachers of color that could not demonstrate success when working with students of color also had a minimalistic view of culturally responsive practice or multicultural education and a somewhat deficit mindset of students of color.

Further, what is often not talked about is that teachers of color also have challenges to face when working with students who are immigrants or different languages, even when the skin tone of the students is brown. The students of color surveyed for this book mentioned some challenges with teachers of color who were not of their same race or ethnicity. While these teachers of color connected with these students of color better than White teachers, they did not connect with them at the same level that teachers of their same race or ethnicity did.

What is evident here is that teachers of color also need training and professional development in working with students who are different. It may seem that being marginalized themselves, they would be able to understand the differences students bring to the classroom. However, just as with White teachers, if there is no experience with students who are different in the midst of a large group of students who have multiple similarities, it may be even challenging for teachers of color. So, what are the differences between these challenged teachers of color and other, more successful teachers of color mentioned throughout this book?

The commonalities of the teachers mentioned throughout this book are that these teachers build positive relationships with students and communities, are self-reflective and honest with themselves, believe in culturally responsive lessons and student behaviors, empathize with the challenges students face, are patient and resilient, advocate for justice, and believe in students. Further, these teachers constantly seek professional development or a higher degree of education. This is why the emphasis of this book is on successful teachers of color.

LOCAL AND STATE CHALLENGES IN DIVERSIFYING TEACHER EDUCATION

As school districts, states, and even the nation looks to diversify the educator workforce, the field must take a critical, realistic, and strategic look at how to move the workforce in this direction. Some of the efforts to diversify teacher education are centered on grow-your-own or pathway programs. (This will be covered in greater detail in the next chapter.) Yet the educational system must understand its diverse population and assess whether the district or state has an efficient diverse population to transform its educational system.

For instance, when looking at 2013 data from *Teacher Diversity Matters*, it was found that there was a gap between the percentage of teachers of color in a state and students of color in a state, ranging from a 4 percent difference to a 43 percent difference. The states with a smaller difference in the percentage between teachers and students of color were states with a small population of color such as Maine, Vermont, West Virginia, and New Hampshire. The states with the largest difference in the gap between teachers and students of color were places with a larger population of color such as California, Nevada, Texas, New York, and Arizona.

Additionally, there were more than twenty states that had a gap between teachers and students of color of 25 percent or greater. A correlation was run on the data to see if there was a statistical link between the percentage in the teachers/students of color gap and the Black/White and Latinx/White achievement gap for each state using the National Assessment of Educational Progress Eighth-Grade data. The basic thought here was to show if having a greater diverse teaching pool could reduce the achievement gap among these populations.

There was a statistically significant correlation found, meaning those states with a larger gap between their teacher and student of color populations had a larger gap in the achievement scores of their Black and Latinx students in comparison to their White students. The findings also showed that having a smaller teacher/student of color gap reduced the achievement gap between White students and students of color. These findings further emphasize the impact of having a diverse educator workforce.

This also supports the findings of research on ethnic matching, which shows that teachers of color have a significant impact on the academic outcomes of students of color. Upon further examination, what was noticed was that there were four states (Vermont, Maine, West Virginia, and New Hampshire) that had the lowest teachers/students of color gap: less than 10 percent. Also, these states have the lowest populations of color in the United States. This led to an examination of states with a small population of color; could these states reduce the teacher/student of color gap?

The difference between the teacher/student gap and the percentage of adults of color in the state was calculated to create an index to determine if there were enough adults in each state to cover the teacher/student gap. Afterward, another correlation was run and showed a statistically significantly strong positive relationship. These findings imply that the greater the percentage of the adults of color in a state, the higher the teacher/student of color gap.

For example, Texas's people of color population is 55 percent and the difference in their student/teacher population is 32 percent. Therefore, the gap between teacher/student of color and the percentage of adults of color in the state is 23. These findings suggest that the difference in the student/teacher population of Texas is greater than 23 percent of the overall state population, which means Texas has more than enough adults of color to train as teachers.

On the other hand, when looking at the difference in the population of color and teacher/student of color gap for Nebraska, the finding is −4 percent. These findings propose that the state of Nebraska does not have enough adults of color in the state to cover the 22 percent student/teacher of color gap in their public schools. These findings follow the logic of the National Education Association, which proposed one of the dilemmas of recruiting teachers of color: "Demographically, a region, state, or school district contains few minorities locally available for its teacher pool."

Other findings show that among those states with less than a 25 percent adult of color population, the gap between the combination of teacher/student of color gap and adults of color gap in the state ranged from −4 to 0. This suggests that states like Maine, Vermont, Iowa, and South Dakota do not have enough of an adult of color population to cover the gap between their teachers and students of color. Of those states, about 26 to 40 percent ranged between 3 and 9 percent. These states might have a marginal chance of bringing adults of color into the field of education and should consider a grow-your-own program, as they may have significant competition from other fields looking to diversify.

States with an adult population of color 41 percent and higher ranged between 10 and 59 percent. These states—California, South Carolina, Hawaii, Texas, and others—were among the states with the largest people of color population. They should have no problem diversifying their teaching pool.

These findings indicate that states with a larger student/teacher gap in the school population of color are experiencing these gaps between the school and their connection with their populations of color. Meanwhile, one of the critical strategies for increasing the academic success of students of color is by engaging these students with more teachers of color.

TEACHER PREPARATION PROGRAMS

Over the years, teacher preparation programs have been limited in recruiting and graduating teachers of color. It could very well be because teacher preparation programs are led by predominantly White faculty.[6] As a substitute, teacher education programs have leaned on culturally responsive practice and pedagogy as a proxy for developing a diverse educator workforce.

Legendary scholar Dr. Christine Sleeter proposes that teacher education programs, while speaking the language of social justice, are continuing to graduate predominantly White teachers. In turn, these programs are not preparing White teachers to respond in a culturally responsive matter when teaching students of color. As this book has shown, educational preparation programs also are not as effective in recruiting and graduating teachers of color.

Yet one of the critical findings of this book is that there is a disconnect between White teachers and students of color. As indicated earlier, teacher preparation programs may contribute to this disconnect in the way in which culturally responsive teaching or multicultural education is taught. This is not to suggest that White teachers are bad teachers or that they are not understanding culturally responsive practice. It does, however, lead one to wonder if the way in which culturally responsive practice taught in teacher preparation programs is intentional, meaningful, and deliberate.

The findings in this book echo the lack of effective culturally responsive training on the teacher preparation level. Again, when looking at why teachers of color respond to students of color in a culturally responsive matter and with attention to the cultural environment and needs of students, teachers of color were asked to share the practices in their teacher preparation program that aided them in working with students of color. The teachers overwhelmingly responded that they did not receive much or any training on working with students of color or in culturally responsive education.

In their programs, some teachers felt that multicultural education and culturally responsive practice was taught in theory, but not as an "application." For example, a Latina teacher who taught in a small town with a student of color population over 50 percent and a 30 percent teacher of color population, explained that in her bilingual education program, she learned to work with language learners but was never taught to work with students of color.

While language learners tend to be students of color, she was never taught how to differentiate or connect the cultures of students as a way to better know her students, build relationships, and establish trust with her students. She explained that it took a personal desire to know more about her students and their cultural practices for her to be a more effective teacher. By reconnecting with her students in a way that demonstrated that she understood who they were, she felt she learned so much from her students and felt a reconnection to the practice of education.

Beyond this book, there are a number of professors and scholars, both of color and White, who have been able to move students and motivate them to work effectively with students of color. These professionals are intentional, meaningful, and deliberate in their approach about culturally responsive practice and working with diverse student populations.

For instance, high school students in the Oregon Teacher Pathway program were introduced to various scholars whose focus was on culturally responsive practice. They engaged with the likes of Dr. Geneva Gay, Dr. Rich Milner, Dr. Christine Sleeter, and Dr. Jeff Duncan-Andrade. The message these high school students received literally changed their lives. These students were presented with an approach to education they had never had before. The messages they received hit home with them.

After meeting Dr. Geneva Gay, a cohort felt compelled to do a culturally responsive workshop for *hir* teachers. After meeting Dr. Rich Milner, weeks would go by and students would be seen with his book, marked up from beginning to end; they constantly quoted his book as if he was a preacher coming to save teacher education. After a Skype conversation with Dr. Jeff Duncan-Andrade, students first felt honored that he would speak to them, and they were moved to tears because they felt humanized, empowered, and uplifted by him. With Dr. Christine Sleeter, the students were surprised to see a White scholar speak with so much passion and depth about culturally responsive education.

Many of these teachers who taught the dual credit course felt that they learned more about working with students of color through actual experience with students and through professional development held by their school district. These teachers valued being able to learn how to work with students of color while at the same time being able to put what they learned into practice.

Given that some of these teachers felt that they did not receive much culturally responsive training in their college programs, there is something about these teachers that gives them the energy and motivation to want to be successful with students of color rather than finding the job difficult and stepping away from the profession. Here, these teachers talked about the value of building relationships with their students.

One teacher explained that if the students knew that their teachers cared about them and were interested in them, teachers would have more time to spend teaching them and less time managing problems in the classroom. The teacher mentioned that if teachers can show a level of compassion for their students, the students will essentially do anything for them in the classroom. These opinions offer an alternative view to many teachers of color in urban communities who were somehow made to feel that teaching is a difficult chore in which they are not valued but are told to just do their job.

To better understand the role of teacher preparation programs and the relationship between teachers and students of color, data received from teachers were again examined to understand the effectiveness of teacher preparation programs. Again, looking back on the original fifty-two teachers interviewed for this book, the thirty-two that could not demonstrate success when working with students of color had a minimalistic view of culturally responsive practice or multicultural education and somewhat deficit mindset of students of color.

These teachers could not talk about what made them successful teachers. In a conversation with legendary scholar Dr. Geneva Gay about these findings, she proposed that it is important not to overinterpret these findings, as sometimes preservice teachers, teachers, and other educators can effectively engage and work with students of color. However, at some level, the information presented to individual teachers is not being conveyed in a way that can lead them to carry out effective practices.

On the other hand, some successful teachers just work with students without thinking in terms of the effectiveness of what they do; they simply do the work, and their cultural responsiveness is just innate. However, here there was no one thing to point to that showed evidence of successful teaching.

In presenting how they were effective in their practice with students of color, teachers who came from master's of arts in teaching (MAT) programs with strong commitments to social justice in practice—programs such as Teach Tomorrow in Oakland and university programs like the Institute for Urban Education at the University of Missouri–Kansas City as well as the Kansas City Teacher Residency Program—were much more able to speak with passion about working with students of color. It was also these teachers who had a strong desire to further their own education.

On the other hand, teachers from traditional university-based programs and alternative programs could speak about social justice and culturally responsive practice but could not translate these approaches into practice. These findings are in no way meant to assign a level of quality to these particular programs; but it would be great to see these programs have a positive impact on students, because a significant number of teachers of color come from these types of programs. More importantly, the findings show that teacher preparation programs of all types are not preparing White teachers or teachers of color to work effectively with a diverse student population.

A rationale presented by Dr. Rich Milner is that 78 percent of teacher education program faculty members are White. This is not to imply that White faculty cannot teach culturally responsive education. However, it is possible that these faculty members do not have an intimate understanding of the challenges students of color/diverse groups face. It is not certain that these particular faculty members would be effective in teaching culturally responsive or multicultural education through the critical cultural lens needed for working with diverse student populations.

As proposed in previous chapters, the knowledge that students bring to a situation comes from a cultural and historical interpretation of experiences or events. Information is better analyzed by individuals communicating with others. However, if individuals communicate with people of similar mindsets or cultural frameworks, they may develop an unconscious cultural bias of experiences or events. In order to understand a situation totally, one has to truly understand the lived experiences of others. This can only happen if one allows *hirself* to totally be open with accepting others' narratives as truth while at the same time not feeling that *hir* truths are being threatened.

TAKEAWAYS

The US educational system is at a tipping point in which the landscape of public school students is more diverse in language, race/ethnicity, and economic level.[7] Additionally, communities are finding that the students and teachers in their schools did not necessarily grow up in a common community. So communities are having to reevaluate the way in which they approach the needs for their schools. However, this should not be left only to schools, teachers, and principals to figure out. All stakeholders responsible for our educational system must come together to promote system design with a goal of providing culturally responsive quality teachers to all students.

As we have seen, there are a number of challenges facing the field of education. As presented in this chapter and throughout the book, the increase of a more diverse school system is one of our greatest challenges facing today's schools. Also, as mentioned, diversifying the educator workforce is key to reducing stress on students, teachers, educational systems, and community. Other challenges facing the field are (1) finding enough people of color interested in becoming teachers, to satisfy states' needs, (2) retaining teachers of color, and (3) creating an educational system take produces culturally responsive teachers regardless of race/ethnicity.

To accomplish this, again, all educational units, including teacher preparation programs, school districts, policy makers, and other stakeholders have to work together to understand the value of diversifying the educator workforce. They must develop training and continuous professional development designed to support a diverse workforce community for both students and professionals, and engage in educational reform that pushes the need for a system that includes culturally responsive practice and that exists beyond urban Black and Latinx communities.

Chapter 7

Systematic Strategies for Developing a More Diverse and Culturally Responsive Workforce

I create a classroom atmosphere that is welcoming and perceptive. Perceptive and conscious of needs that extend beyond academics. I am an educator not afraid to deviate from the script. I focus on meeting my students where they are and giving them what they need to be successful and often that is not included in the state-based standards. My data scores are often the highest among my colleagues on my grade level (for whatever that means).

—*Black teacher, Washington, DC*

Importance in the work of diversifying the educator workforce is that it is not solely the responsibility of teachers or teacher preparation programs or school districts. It takes a collective effort to develop a rich, diverse, and quality educator workforce. This chapter will present some systematic strategies used by states, universities, and districts to diversify the educator workforce and to enhance culturally responsive skills of all teachers.

With this, it is important for the field of education at all levels to understand and embrace the critical challenges facing schools as communities are transforming and becoming more diverse at an increasingly rapid rate. Consequently, this transformation brings with it a complexity of diverse factors that may have a critical impact on the function and structure of the systematic nature of the schools.

There are communities in the United States, both rural and urban, that have seen drastic changes to their districts over a three- to five-year span. Brought to districts are the need for English-language-learner instruction and in some cases the need to develop Title 1 schools and instruction. Further, as these students migrate into predominantly White school districts, they still bring with them a cultural lens. It can understandably be challenging for schools, but it will be more challenging for schools to force these students to assimilate into the school culture. In a diverse learning community, the environment must engage in culturally responsive strategies for that system to work effectively.

POLICIES AND DIVERSIFYING TEACHER EDUCATION

As mentioned throughout this book, the US student of color population is expected to represent more than half of the students in US public schools by 2025, with no sign that there will be the same growth in numbers of teachers of color. In an effort to create a stronger teacher workforce, the US Department of Education under the Obama administration developed the Every Student Succeeds Act (ESSA), a policy established to partially increase the number of educators of color.

ESSA places a commitment to equity and diversity by providing an opportunity for all states to include in their plans the ways that they will address gaps in the educator workforce as well as in student achievement. In addition to providing autonomy and flexibility to state governments, ESSA suggests increases in federal and state investments in high-quality education programs at HBCUs, Hispanic-serving institutions (HSIs), Asian American and Native American/Pacific Islander-serving institutions, Tribal colleges and universities, and public colleges and universities serving large numbers of students of color.

Often left out of major discussions concerning the educator workforce, ESSA has provided a space for people of color–serving institutions. Further, ESSA seeks federal and state support in developing and expanding programs that show evidence of helping to recruit, mentor, and support teachers of color.

Prior to the implementation of ESSA, Oregon, among a few other states, took the initiative and began developing plans to diversify the teacher workforce. Around 2010 Oregon saw that it was experiencing a more rapid growth in its population of color than any other state on the Pacific coast. The state started seeing an extreme change both in urban and rural school communities. Between 2010 and 2017, the state witnessed its student of color population grow from 25 percent to 37 percent across thirty-one districts. Prior to 2010, the state created the Oregon Minority Report to help guide districts in understanding diversity across the state.

Given the new changes in its schools' demographics, the Oregon Department of Education supported the development of the Oregon Educator Advisory Group by Dr. Hilda Rosselli and chaired by Dr. Donald Easton-Brooks. The group comprised a twenty-member community of various stakeholders, including school leaders, teachers, community leaders, com-munity organizations, higher-education personnel, state legislators, and non-profit organizations. The work of the group was to diversify education at all levels and focus on efforts from the classroom to higher education.

With this, the group worked with various state education agencies and community stakeholders to change the name of the Oregon Minority Teacher Report to the Oregon Educator Equity Report to reflect the current state of the state in response to equitable education practices. The Advisory Group was charged with developing a state plan for meeting the goals established by the Educator Equity Report.

The original charge was to monitor the state's progress toward the goals established by the former Oregon Minority Teacher Act by (1) regularly evalu-ating progress and results for Oregon recruitment, preparation, professional development, and retention initiatives addressing the shortage of culturally and linguistically diverse educators; (2) reviewing data compiled for the Oregon Educator Equity Report; and (3) making specific recommendations on needed practices and policies to the Chief Education Officer.

Based on the changes and the growing need in the state, the charge was developed to (1) research, coordinate, and oversee legislative reports deriving from Oregon's current status and progress toward diversifying the educator workforce, and spotlight/recommend/drive needed practices and policies; (2) ensure that the voices of culturally and linguistically diverse citizens in Oregon are engaged in examining root causes, current assets, and needed changes in policy and practices that can help diversify Oregon's educator workforce; (3) review progress and results from state-funded investments intended to recruit, prepare, retain, and advance Oregon's educator work-force; and (4) recommend future investments for the state that can improve students' access to educators who more closely mirror their K–12 student population demographics.

Based on this charge, the group produces an annual report that includes a summary of most recent data on diversity in Oregon's educator workforce. The report offers practices for recruiting, preparing, hiring, and retaining culturally and linguistically diverse educators; plans that were implemented by public schools; and recommendations that the educator workforce closely mirror Oregon's K–12 student demographics.

Results from the efforts of the group show that the state reportedly employed 10.1 percent culturally or linguistically diverse teachers, which is a 5.5 percent increase since 2015–2016. They also reported that since 2011–2012, districts have increased the number of ethnically diverse teachers hired in Oregon Public Schools by 21 percent. Since 2014–2015, there has also been a 20 percent increase in the number of linguistically and ethnically diverse teachers employed in Oregon Public Schools.

Given the group's focus on educators of all levels, they now have an 11 percent administrators of color population, and 18 percent paraeducators of color population, and 13 percent guidance counselors of color population. The state has also seen a significant (10 percent) growth in candidates of color as teacher preparation program completers since the first report in 2014–2015. The efforts in Oregon are a snapshot of a strong proactive push to ensure educational equity through a diverse educator workforce plan.

Key to Oregon is that the state has strategically looked at ways to work with various agencies, both public and private, to ensure equity across the state. However, Oregon needs to remain vigilant. The state should caution against pushing schools to quantify the number of teachers of color needed by a particular date, as this might unintentionally encourage school leaders to make quick hiring decisions and select unprepared teachers. Hiring must be strategic with a robust training and retaining plan. Also, schools must not place unrealistic expectations on teachers of color as they enter the workforce, such as using them to "save" students of color.

SCHOOL LEADERS AND DIVERSE SCHOOLING

Another systematic factor in developing a more diverse workforce resides in school-level leaders. Beyond teachers, school leaders are important in influencing the academic lives of students of color. They are critical in establishing and setting the tone for learning and teaching as well as for valuing equity, diversity, and inclusion. Within and outside of diverse school settings, this work can be challenging. Contributing to the challenge are the various perceptions for various stakeholders on equity, diversity, and inclusion. Therefore, the school leader must show the depth to which *ze* is able to move the school to function within a diverse and inclusive framework.

It is easy to develop a mindset that a diverse workforce matters only in schools with large numbers of students of color. Still, a diverse workforce is equally as important in racially homogenous settings and majority White schools. Similarly, among interracial interactions and socialization beyond school, White students and students of color both benefit from attending schools with one another. Therefore, it is important for school leaders to build school cultures in which all students are valued and develop interactions that continue to grow both inside and outside of schools and classrooms.

Culturally responsive leaders' see developing a culturally responsive school climate as an opportunity rather than a challenge. They are more often than not transformative leaders who look at this work as an opportunity to harmonize the school and offer all children equitable educational opportunities and high-quality schooling. Through intervention efforts, these leaders strive to counter marginalizing forces. As such, they engage in self-reflection, systematic analysis of schools, and confrontation of inequities regarding race, class, gender, language, ability, and/or sexual orientation.

Like the responsive teachers mentioned in chapter 5, these leaders take on the charge of intentional and culturally responsive practice, challenge the status quo, and work toward the cultural transformation of schooling. Further, these leaders work both inside schools to promote culturally responsive practice and within communities to promote equity and inclusion.

These leaders value the importance of culturally responsive practices such that they would challenge school board members and district leaders to consider more broadly responsive practice. These leaders are needed to help improve more policies and practices while adopting equity-based curricula and committing to hiring a more diverse workforce. They are often more capable of promoting and sustaining an environment stable enough to attract, maintain, and support the future development of good teachers.

GROW-YOUR-OWN PROGRAMS

Grow-your-own (GYO) programs have been viewed as the current model for diversifying teacher education. There are various forms and variations of these programs. There are pathway programs that are school-based, university-school–based programs, and nonprofit/private, organizationally based programs. However, the challenge of GYOs has to do with their approach.

As proposed at the beginning of this chapter, all work must be a collaborative effort, but this statement must be amended a bit. These collaborative efforts must focus on the historical research around culturally responsive practice/multicultural education and critical conversations of race, class, and other oppressive labels within the day-to-day practice of schools. These efforts must be centered on more supportive policies and practices in these areas.

Proposed in this book are the attributes of culturally responsive practice. These attributes are based on research by Dr. James Banks, Dr. Gloria Ladson-Billings, and Dr. Geneva Gay and provide an evidence-based framework for engaging in culturally responsive teaching and practice. GYOs that do not include some element of research-based culturally responsive practice should be questioned as to the level of their intentionality; such programs may have not taken to heart the value and purpose of culturally responsive practice as it has been studied over the past few decades.

Programs such as Pathways2Teaching (P2T), Oregon Teacher Pathways (OTP), the University of South Dakota (USD) Teacher Pathway Program, Call Me Mister, and IMPACT are GYO programs that are culturally responsive and research-based.[1,2,3,4] The P2T, created by Dr. Margarita Bianco at the University of Colorado–Denver, and the OTP at Eastern Oregon University (based the P2T model) are high school GYO programs. P2T is focused more on urban communities, and OTP is focused more on rural and small-town communities.

Both P2T and OTP programs work in partnership with area school districts and are designed to recruit, educate, and graduate students of color who are interested in becoming teachers. The goal of the programs is to respond to the needs of our schools by training culturally responsive teachers who are capable of working with students and families from various diverse backgrounds. The programs begin with training high school students in their junior and senior years by offering these students a chance to take dual-credit college-level courses in introduction to education and culturally responsive practice.

The students in P2T and OTP are involved in a one-hour-per-week field experience in which they tutor elementary school students. This gives students the opportunity to see the impact they can have on a person's learning by helping children develop their reading or mathematics skills. The students also have the opportunity to work with college professors and mentors. An exciting part of the program for students is that they have a chance to interact with leading scholars in the field of culturally responsive practice.

Along with meeting scholars in the field, the students also conduct research on topics related to culturally responsive practice. In both P2T and OTP, students were not selected based on GPA. Students were selected if they showed interest in the program or were recommended by a teacher, school leaders, or community leaders. In the OTP program, attendance of the students increased and their grades improved. More importantly, one of the elementary schools with a large Mexican population saw the test scores of many of their elementary students, who were tutored by OTP high school students, go from not meeting standards to meeting or exceeding standards.

Many of the OTP students got to see the real impact teachers could have on the lives of students. Some of the students talked about taking what they learned in the program and being able to help and empower their young siblings or cousins. What was most critical was that after these students had learned more about culturally responsive practice, they became more confident and empowered. OTP would not have happened if it were not for state initiatives in recruiting and retaining teachers of color through the Oregon Department of Education, which funded six initiatives across the state in an effort to diversify teacher education and to build a strong, culturally responsive educator workforce.

Similar to P2T and OTP, the USD School of Education created a Pathway program with the Sioux Falls School District. The district has seen major increases in its populations of color. As a way to connect with their schools, the leaders of the district and the leaders of the School of Education formed a partnership. However, different from P2T and OTP programs, the USD/ Sioux Falls partnership started with year-long conversations and training at the district and school leadership levels, facilitated by faculty in the School of Education.

The point here was to discuss how to address culturally responsive practices in the classrooms. These meetings led to the forming of a think tank facilitated and led by Dr. Derrick Robinson, which explored concepts and strategies related to culturally responsive school leadership and culturally responsive pedagogy. A year later, the think tank agreed to pilot a semester-long culturally responsive workforce initiative with four schools.

The initiative consisted of workshops/professional developments targeting school leaders and teachers. Professional development focused on culturally responsive school leadership practices designed for school leaders, counselors, instructional coaches, and admin interns; and on culturally responsive pedagogy designed for school teachers. The workshop consisted of four four-hour sessions with activities between sessions. During the pilot, several activities, including pre- and posttest surveys, were done to collect data on key areas of focus for future usage in relation to the strategic initiative.

The surveys produced areas of growth. At the leadership level, the survey showed various areas for growth. One was that leadership should *improve communication with parents and communities* by rethinking the district's communication process and developing strategies to grow situational awareness for improving communications in various communities. In addition, leaders should *be prepared for critical conversations on race, gender, and class.*

The conversation here centered on school leaders' recognition of their responsibility to engage in conversations with teachers about race, gender, and class, and to set policies and practices around the way schools and the district engaged in culturally responsive practice. Another level to this training included developing culturally responsive teachers as described on the intentionality scale mentioned in chapter 5. Here, the school could create workshops to assist teachers to enhance their ability to become more intentional in culturally responsive practices.

The survey also showed that the leaders should *challenge status quo practices* in the district, recognize possible bias perceptions of families and family cultures, and develop strategies for understanding families and family cultures through a cultural lens. To enhance the district's approach to effectively working with students, the school leaders could also engage with district personnel on eliminating marginalizing practices that adversely affect diverse students.

Finally, the survey showed that the leaders should *improve self-awareness and self-reflection.* As the district is new to more diverse learning communities, leaders in the district are faced with enhancing the district so as to effectively engage with its growing diverse populations. The district has a 33 percent student of color population, over two thousand English-language learners, and eighty-six different languages spoken in the district. Therefore, the school leaders have to increase their cultural self-awareness and their awareness of their positioning as leaders in promoting intentional, culturally responsive practices.

On the teacher level, the survey found the following areas for growth: *culturally linguistic knowledge, culturally linguistic examination, cultural responsiveness and interdisciplinary teaching,* and *student importance and inclusion in the classroom.* These constructs centered on teachers' ability to work with diverse language learners and to create a learning environment that is responsive to cultural differences.

Other strategies discussed in the think tank were to extend the culturally responsive workforce initiative to an entire year, develop a summer retreat that focuses on cultural responsiveness in leadership and teaching, integrate cultural responsiveness into new teacher and new leader induction processes, develop and integrate principles of culturally responsive school leadership and culturally responsive pedagogy into the local evaluation and walkthrough instrument, and extend the focus of the work beyond the piloted schools.

Finally, as universities and others engage in GYOs, it is also critical that these programs develop a strong framework for culturally responsive practices as it relates to the mission and vision of the educational unit. The critical reason for this framework is that this work is intentional and should be ever-present in the minds of students, faculty, and other interested parties. This framework should also be used to guide an educational unit's work around culturally responsive pedagogy and assist the unit as it partners with schools to create a diverse teacher pathway program.

An example here is the culturally responsive reflective practice framework developed by the yearlong residency program at USD, as the unit engages in its pathway program with Sioux Falls School District. Here, *culturally responsive reflective practice* is described as educators teaching in a way that demonstrates culturally conscious and reflective practices. In this process, teachers are inclusive, are influenced by, and participate in the cultures (linguistic, racial, ethnic, economic, social, and ability-based) of students in the classroom, school, and community.

The four elements of culturally responsive reflective practice are *culturally responsive learning and instruction, culturally aware relationships, culturally active communication*, and *culturally engaged environment.* These elements align with the core conceptual framework of the unit and are applicable to culturally responsive and multicultural education practices as presented by Dr. James Banks, Dr. Gloria Ladson-Billings, Dr. Geneva Gay, and others. These elements are used to guide conversations and develop a common language culture throughout the partnership. Training is also provided to all parties on the best ways to implement, and best uses of, the framework as a whole and the elements associated with the framework.

Furthermore, what makes the P2T, OPT, and USD Diversity Teacher Pathway programs effective is their development and use of a culturally responsive framework to guide their practices. These frameworks keep this work intentional, impactful, and aligned with creating effective, culturally responsive educators. Without a culturally responsive framework, programs are producing teachers in a culturally unresponsive setting that does not effectively take into account the needs of diverse student populations.

RETENTION OF TEACHERS OF COLOR

As mentioned earlier in this book, over a span of a few decades, the percentage of teachers of color has become more than double the percentage of White teachers entering the field.[5] Yet, these teachers have also left the field at a greater rate than White teachers. So, as the field puts a great effort into recruiting teachers of color, there is a lot of work to do to keep teachers and educators of color in the field at all levels.

One of the big mistakes made is bringing in teachers of color and expecting that they will immediately resolve challenges students of color face. This was relevant to a new teacher of color who went to teach in a highly diverse school. While the teacher desired to make an impact on the students in her school, she felt the immediate pressure of being a teacher working with a large Black population with few teachers of color. Being a first-year teacher, she had little time to go through the basic process normal teachers go through in their first year.

This teacher became overwhelmed with the expectations of being a new teacher and at the same time being saddled with the responsibility of increasing the academic performance of Black students in the school. On multiple levels, this teacher was set up to fail. This is a common occurrence among young teachers of color. They are often expected to take on extra duties and responsibility associated with working with students of color.

This happens because schools are in need of diverse teachers but are not yet equipped to understand the basic needs of teachers, particularly young teachers of color, and of their own setting relative to having a culturally responsive environment. This is why the work with Sioux Falls Schools was critical. Teachers of color go into the profession wanting to advocate for students, but often the schools/districts have not reformed to address the needs of these teachers or the needs of the schools to be inclusive to the point that teachers of color do not carry the weight of the schools' concerns with how to address a diverse student population.

Schools have to move beyond just wanting a diverse workforce. Schools have to want a work environment that is truly inclusive on both the student and teacher level. This includes providing training for a diverse teacher workforce and valuing input from all those who are part of a diverse teacher workforce. While many schools, districts, and states speak of diversity, equity, and inclusion, do they incorporate strategies to measure whether they are effective in these areas? For instance, many districts boldly display equity in their vision, but does the vision extend beyond their website?

This lack of strong policies and practices on equity, diversity, and inclusion as a whole can weigh on the district's ability to retain a strong and diverse workforce. This may be the reason many teachers of color leave the field. While framed as lack of administrative support, it may very well be the lack of administrative knowledge related to developing an inclusive environment in which both culturally responsive practices and effective instructional practice exist together.

What may also be missing in this conversation is the lack of credibility given to these teachers. In conversations with some of color, those who are licensed have mentioned the lack of interview opportunities, not being hired after an interview, and feeling that their knowledge and ability are not credible. A teacher of color once complained after being hired in a district in which she brought four years of experience, her peers questioned her ability and her principal was constantly visiting her classroom.

The teacher never had parental complaints, and test scores at the end of the year were level with the other teachers at her grade level. Needless to say, the teacher did not return to the district. An added challenge is the institutional racism felt by teachers toward students of color that is directly or indirectly extended to these teachers. When not dealing with judgments related to their credibility, more teachers of color, especially in low-income communities, face the challenge of the unnecessarily harsh treatment of students of color.

These teachers, especially males of color, are often made or looked to as disciplinarians of students of color, which reduces their time for lesson planning and other prep related to learning. To combat this inequity on many levels, the National Education Association (NEA) has devoted $7 million to increase equity opportunity for both teachers and students and to address issues related to institutional racism.

So what is the solution for retaining teachers of color? One answer is to stop doing what has been done to push these teachers out of the profession. It can be suggested that what students of color have experienced for years, the lack of an educational system that is reflective of their educational needs through a culturally engaging curriculum is the same thing that teachers of color are facing in the profession.

It has been mentioned throughout this book that teachers of color engage in teaching mainly as a way to support and promote successful learning opportunities for students of color. Then they see a system that remains challenging for these students, and they experience similar challenges on the professional level; they see a system that is broken with no signs of changing. Those teachers of color who stay in the profession either work around these challenges, become part of a system of simply managing the behaviors of these students, or truly work within a system that is responsive to learning through a culturally responsive lens.

As we hope for the latter to be true, it is vital that school and district leaders at all levels take a more active approach in understanding and developing a climate that is receptive to teachers of color. As it is known that students of color are more dependent on teachers of color for their success, leaders will need to reform schools to be more welcoming to both students and teachers of color.

From a systematic and strategic framework, leaders have to focus on a system that is equitable, culturally responsive, and inclusive. In this, the system must give and train all teachers to teach and bring to the profession a cultural lens—that is, provide these teachers with an unbiased opportunity to teach. This means that the system must be open to looking at schooling through a lens that may not be familiar to them.

For instance, a Black former assistant principal shared the challenge of a school undergoing a major demographic shift from a predominantly White to a predominantly Black student population, which created a cultural mismatch between the teacher and student populations. The school went from 27 percent to 58 percent Black and from 23 percent to 55 percent free or reduced lunch.

This change also had an impact on the academic status of the school. Once a School of Distinction, with close to 90 percent of its students at grade level, the school witnessed academic achievement test scores of students go from 85 percent to 15 percent in algebra, 93 percent to 48 percent in English, and 92 percent to 48 percent in biology. Over a year, the challenges took a toll on teachers and leadership, and the school experienced rapid turnover. However, in the midst of all of this, teachers and the pedagogical approach they used in the school had not changed to respond to new and different learners.

In an attempt to right the ship, the school hired a Black assistant principal. However, in the same way as some schools expect Black teachers to come in, be disciplinarians, and "get the Black students in shape," the new leader received similar comments. He expressed that he was eagerly ready to engage with staff to redirect culture and achievement, but teachers were more concerned with discipline and containment of children rather than instruction. And many teachers were not as eager for change, as they saw the school as having more disciplinary problems than academic problems.

The assistant principal mentioned that there was a mixture of attitudes among teachers, with some teachers of color committed to culturally responsive practice and some teachers of color who were deficit-based (much like the teachers mentioned in chapter 5), and White teachers who were either committed, asset-based, stuck, or deficit-based. Many of the teachers in the school were focused on content but not on culturally responsive practices. Many teachers lowered their efforts in planning and delivering quality instruction on the belief that their students could not or were unwilling to learn.

Even when presented with culturally responsive instructional suggestions, these teachers acknowledged that the ideas were great but would never work for their students. This low teacher expectancy impacted the climate, behavior, and dynamic of teachers and administration and contributed to the social and mental stress of the students. The assistant principal mentioned that it was a challenge to organize and lead deficit-based, culturally mismatched teachers to be more responsive and engaged with diverse students of color. He first attempted to find ways to engage and empower staff agency in hopes that it would transfer into greater student achievement.

When the teachers were challenged to address achievement data and overall instructional improvement, the conversations almost immediately turned to student-based reasons that the scores were low, such as behavior and skill deficits. The lesson the former assistant principal described was that leading and teaching through a transition into a culturally responsive environment is a process, and leaders and teachers' failure to go through the process only serves to strain the achievement and success of students and communities and the teachers and leaders themselves. Increasingly, diverse student bodies present a prime opportunity for school leaders to integrate cultural responsiveness as a natural extension of teaching and leading practices.

Should future teachers and leaders continue on the path of traditional preparation and practice, the development of the responsiveness needed to guide schools through transition will be left to chance and natural ability. Better to establish a foundation for the infusion of cultural responsiveness in the preparation phase of teacher and leader development. As future teachers and leaders of color and their White counterparts transition into practice, the value of their training and dispositions will prove monumental in how they act to guide schools through culture-based transitions of their own.

TAKEAWAYS

In support of diversifying teacher education, ESSA legislation provides states an opportunity to use federal funds to support pathways for diversifying teacher education. This plan should be applauded, as this effort is needed to help states focus on making plans for responding to and creating more equitable educational systems, especially given that we are seeing many of our public schools transform into highly ethnically diverse schools overnight.

These changes are forcing all communities to reexamine schooling for a more diverse student population. Based on research conducted over the past decade, we know that teachers of color can have a significant impact on the educational outcomes of students of color and the educational community as a whole. Therefore, the ESSA is correct in pushing states into looking for strategies to enhance educational systems for *all* students.

However, what is scary is that in this attempt, we might see the numbers of teachers of color going up and quality sacrificed for the pure sake of numbers. The educational leaders may say they want "quality," in words, but their policies must do something other than produce what the "system" wants: simply more teachers of color. If this should happen, the new teachers of color, if not trained correctly, will continue to fail these students. In turn, our students of color will continue to lag behind academically.

Related to ESSA, consider the difference between two national meetings addressing the topic of diversifying teacher education through ESSA. It was a tale of two meetings: One meeting was successful as the group looked to address the current challenges and the challenges ahead. The other meeting was more politically motivated, filled with nonprofits convincing states to let them help create systems to diversify teacher education. Young professionals from nonprofits with no background in the work of diversifying teaching, culturally responsive practice, or teacher education ran the meeting.

These were organizations that mostly collaborate with nonprofit teacher preparation programs that produce less than 20 percent of teachers of color. While institutions of higher education (IHEs), especially HBCUs and HSIs, produce a higher percentage of teachers of color, they still need and should do more, and perhaps more importantly, they need to be at the table for these conversations. As mentioned, this work must be done in collaboration with and in respect of the many scholars who have engaged in this work over the past few decades.

The reality is that the work needed to increase the number of quality teachers and leaders of color and to enhance the educational outcomes of students of color must be intentional and purposeful. This is still an understatement. This is hard and critical work because the system must eliminate decades of failure and create a more transformative and reformed educational environment. What is needed is an intentional and robust infrastructure created by IHEs, state-level departments of educations, local communities and schools, and nonprofits who respect and support IHEs in this work and vice versa. This work takes time but is necessary.

Furthermore, rather than promoting more nonprofits, it seems that a more effective move would be to look at systems already in place, to look toward scholars of color who have researched and produced programs for just this purpose. Pathway programs like P2T should be of interest, as should the university-based programs like Call Me Mister, Project IMPACT, and HBCU offerings. There are professional development programs such as the Institute for Teachers of Color Committed to Racial Justice (ITOC) and the Healing, Empowerment, Love, Liberation, and Action (H.E.L.L.A.) grassroots professional development efforts by teachers of color.[6,7,8]

Some states have developed initiatives to address their educational systems, like the Oregon Educator Equity Advisory Group. Other states, like Illinois and Missouri, have similar systems in place. For ESSA to be successful, we need to build the educational infrastructure by looking at already existing programs that are thoughtful, intentional, purposeful, and have been interested in this work since before ESSA came to be.

As the field looks to find ways to diversify our teacher workforce by developing better recruitment and retention strategies, the field must also consider ways to assist both teachers of color and White teachers with practical strategies for motivating students of color. As this book suggests, one of the means to do this is by understanding the practices by successful teachers of color as markers for training preservice teachers, producing effective professional development, and helping districts and higher education programs in reforming students to meet the needs of new, twenty-first-century public schools.

Conclusion

Over the past few decades, scholars like Michele Foster, Geneva Gay, Gloria Ladson-Billings, James Banks, Christine Sleeter, Lisa Delpit, and others have been key in setting the framework on the value and importance of culturally responsive and multicultural education as well as the need for diversifying the field of education. Many present-day scholars have continued building on the foundation of this work. The task of getting the field of education to recognize the value and importance of this work, done over the past few decades, is now among us.

Our schools now are becoming more diverse, and the pattern is expected to continue over the next couple of decades. The challenge here is twofold. First, we can accept that collectively schooling, pedagogy, and practice in this current structure is not effective in meeting the needs of students of color. Second, as our schools continue to become more diverse, we have to find a way to reach the needs of these students.

One of the strategies that has been embraced, at least by many scholars of color, is ethnic matching or pairing of students and teachers of color, which is considered valuable in enhancing these students' experiences. Current research shows that teachers of color are now having a significant impact on the academic experience of White students. With this, it seems logical that the studies of the scholars mentioned above hold weight. There is a critical need to diversify the field of education and to create an educative environment that foundationally embraces culturally responsive and multicultural education.

What can contribute to ethnic matching is that the expectations of students of color by teachers of color can be different from that of White teachers and could be centered on cultural experiences, cultural expectations, and cultural biases. These can lead to explicit, implicit, or situational forms of perceptive expectations. Often, this perception is led by a deficit mindset by the teacher.

To compound matters, a student of color relationship with the teacher could be influenced by a perceptive notion of discrimination. If any of these factors exist, it could cause the student social or mental stress, which could have a lasting effect on *hir* academic ability, learning, and experience.

It is possible for teachers of color to have a deficit mindset about students of color, like other teachers who may have a deficit mindset about these students, this experience can lead to, again, social and mental stress in students. Yet the focus of this book was on successful interactions between students and teachers of color. The belief here is that research shows that teachers of color are successful with students of color and that their positive expectations of students of color are greater than those of White teachers with regard to the same students. Still, a deficit mindset is also possible by teachers of color. Therefore, the central focus of this book was on successful teachers of color.

The framework that has been referenced follows the validity methods used by scholars such as Gloria Ladson-Billings, Michele Forster, Rita Kohi, and Marvin Lynn, among others, who have provided concrete evidence through case studies of the need to diversify and promote culturally responsive practices. This book built on this approach to understand what makes such practices work and see if these findings real. What was discovered or rediscovered was that this work goes beyond believing that diversity and culturally responsive practice is needed in our schools.

While the findings for this book may seem like nothing new to some—as the findings do not contradict what the scholars named above have found—they show that there is a level of intentionality to this work that cannot be faked, one that trumps the pure thought of knowing that culturally responsive practice is needed. Successful teachers of color did more than just "know"; they embraced their students' cultures and needs far beyond what the curriculum and other schooling standards called for.

These teachers showed a connection and belief that culturally responsive practice should be a part of everything that is done in teaching, in the same way a mathematics or English teacher feels that these subjects are essential in the core framework of teaching and learning. These teachers, even if they wanted to, could not think about teaching outside of culturally responsive practice. Also, given the nature and lives of many students of color, they saw advocacy and a social justice lens as crucial to working with their students to the point they were willing to lose their job before they were willing to stop teaching within their framework.

The question often asked of me is, "Then how can you get teachers to teach using this approach?" My response: "How do you get effective teachers to teach mathematics or science?" Often the answer is that they "love the topic" or they "are open to the topic." My response is that teachers have to love or be open to the topic of culturally responsive practice.

Beyond all of this, the things that I discovered the most in doing this work is that having a more diverse workforce is critical at all levels. Connecting with students of color is critical—and not just in a made-for-TV special way or a "White Teachers Save Students of Color by Connecting with Them" way. These ways tend to show a snapshot of success. Rather, it is critical to connect with these students in a way that shows that teachers see their students as an integral part of their teaching and the curriculum.

Also, in the survey with students of color, the findings showed that White teachers in a workforce where at least one-third of the teacher population was of color were better able to connect the curriculum to the students and to connect with the cultural lives of students of color. These teachers either saw how effective teachers of color were with their students or interacted with teachers of color to better understand how to reach their students, or did both.

Furthermore, a strong part of this work involves *culturally responsive intentionality practice*—for example, building positive relationships with students and community; practicing self-reflection; empathizing with the challenges students face, and so forth—centered on the *critical social pedagogy* framework in which teachers take into account the social aspects of and the challenges facing these students and push back on oppression or injustices that may contribute to or cause their students to fail.

The Cultural Responsiveness Intentionality Scale (CRIS) was used to measure the level to which these teachers are committed to this work. The scale hopefully helps teachers and leaders to understand where they may be in their thinking about culturally responsive practice and how intentional they are in this work. The goal here is training on all levels, and professional development could assist in helping teachers perform at the level of a responsive teacher.

Put another way, the goal is to be a teacher who intentionally thinks about *hir* students and their cultural background in every aspect of planning, teaching, assignments, and assessments. It also involves being able to connect with students beyond the classroom, bringing learning to life, and using their students' cultural lens as a technology for promoting learning.

Moreover, as the field strives to become a more diverse workforce, the hope is that this book presented the critical challenges facing this work. One of our challenges is that we face a need for training in culturally responsive practice that is centered on an intentionality framework and is focused on the research of scholars both past and current. Still, many of our candidates both of color and White are not feeling that they are getting from their preparation programs the knowledge needed to be successful culturally responsive teachers.

This may lead to dealing with the reality that many preparation programs, both college-based and nonprofit-based, are staffed by those who may not have experience in culturally responsive practice, do not know the history and research around culturally responsive pedagogy, or are asked to teach the course by the process of elimination because they may have made more mention of multicultural education than others in their program, school, or organization.

While training on how to be a culturally responsive teacher is essential, the field faces challenges beyond preparing teachers. The field is challenged with how to increase its pool of diverse teachers when other industries are also looking to diversify their fields and can offer higher salaries. How can the education field counteract its negative narrative and promote itself as valuable and reputable?

For the most part, the field has been successful in preparing teachers of color over the past few decades. Yet this population has not made a massive footprint on the field. One of the factors may be that the schools are growing at a much quicker rate than the rate at which teachers of color are being turned out. And we do know that the field is losing teachers of color at a rate about 75 percent faster than that of White teachers. Reasons for this loss are based on a number of factors, including dissatisfaction in the workforce, leaders' inability to engage with teachers of color from a culturally responsive position, and simply the idea that teachers of color are not valued as significant partners in educating all students.

Another challenge the field faces is the misperception that the need for teachers of color is a large city/urban issue and that the challenge resides in Black and Latinx communities, even though the US Asian population is one of the fastest growing ethnic groups in the country. This thinking alone shows that we are not concerned with the value of living in a globally diverse society.

Yet we are seeing many of our rural, small-town, and suburban communities becoming diverse and having school populations between 30 to 60 percent of color, which further suggests that teachers of color are needed in all types of communities. Still, as shown in this book, there are many states that lack the population needed to respond to their teacher/student population gaps with regard to students of color.

In concluding this book, we are left with wondering, how committed are we as a field to the needs of our diverse population? We have witnessed a massive exodus of the most powerful ethnic group from our public schools, which leads me to wonder if enough people remain in power to move this work. At this same time, will the many professionals of color who are committed to doing this work have to face another couple of generations before we see true change on the policy and leadership levels?

Again, I applaud ESSA, yet I fear that the policy will bring the same results clothed in a different package. The work that needs to be done is more than about increasing the number of teachers of color in the education workforce. One thing I learned from this work is that in creating a platform for successfully working with students of color, intentionality must be characteristic of teachers, curricula, leaders, and policies. Here, the word "intentional" does not really get to the profundity at which this work must be focused. "Intentional" in this framework means the actions of educators are truly purposeful, deliberate, thoughtful, and all-consuming.

Such educators look to do more than the average because they know that these schools need more than the average. To get to this level of work and expectation, policy makers, school leaders, teachers, preservice teachers, teacher preparation programs, and other educators must transform what they think they know about education and students of color. Systems must be reformed to take on a diverse approach to learning and processing of information. Both learning and the processing of information must embrace students within a framework centered on cultural responsiveness.

Notes

PREFACE

1. Easton-Brooks, D., Lewis, C., & Zhang, Y. (2009). Ethnic-matching: The influence of Black teachers on the reading scores of Black students. *The National Journal of Urban Education & Practice*, *3*(1), 230–243.

CHAPTER 1

1. See an Act to Prohibit the Importation of Slaves into any Port or Place within the Jurisdiction of the United States.

2. Ogbu, J. U. (1992). Understanding cultural diversity and learning. *Educational Researcher, 21*(8), 5–14.

3. Hune, S., & Takeuchi, D. (2008). *Asian Americans in Washington State: Closing their hidden achievement gaps*. Seattle, WA: Commission on Asian Pacific American Affairs.

4. Nguyen, B. M. D., Nguyen, M. H., Teranishi, R. T., & Hune, S. (2015). The hidden academic opportunity gaps among Asian Americans and Pacific Islanders: What disaggregated data reveals in Washington State. National Commission on Asian American and Pacific Islander Research in Education.

5. Hune, S., & Takeuchi, D. (2008). *Asian Americans in Washington State: Closing their hidden achievement gaps*. A report submitted to The Washington State Commission on Asian Pacific American Affairs. Seattle, WA: University of Washington.

6. Eddy, C. M., & Easton-Brooks, D. (2011). Ethnic matching, school placement, and mathematics achievement of African American students from kindergarten through fifth grade. *Urban Education, 46*(6), 1280–1299.

7. Dee, T. S. (2004). Teachers, race, and student achievement in a randomized experiment. *The Review of Economics and Statistics, 86*(1), 195–210.

8. Clewell, B. C., Puma, M. J., & McKay, S. A. (2005, April). *Does it matter if my teacher looks like me? The impact of teacher race and ethnicity on student academic achievement.* Paper presented at the Annual Meeting of the American Educational Research Association, Montreal, Canada.

9. Rimm-Kaufman, S. E., & Pianta, R. C. (2000). An ecological perspective on the transition to kindergarten: A theoretical framework to guide empirical research. *Journal of Applied Developmental Psychology, 21,* 491–511.

10. Sebastian, H.-Y., & Halpin, P. F. (2016). The importance of minority teachers: Student perceptions of minority versus white teachers. *Educational Researcher, 45*(7), 407–420.

CHAPTER 2

1. Hansen, P. (1998). Schooling a European identity: Ethno-cultural exclusion and nationalist resonance within the EU policy of "the European dimension of education," *European Journal of Intercultural Studies, 9*(1), 5–23. Maliepaard, M., Lubbers, M., & Gijsberts, M. (2010). Generational differences in ethnic and religious attachment and their interrelation: A study among Muslim minorities in the Netherlands, *Ethnic and Racial Studies, 33*(3), 451–472.

2. The use of *hir* and *ze* helps break down the walls of gender assumptions.

3. Easton-Brooks, D. (2012). The conceptual context of knowledge. In G. S. Cannella & S. R. Steinberg (Eds.), *Critical qualitative research reader* (pp. 33–42). New York: Peter Lang Publishing.

4. Cacioppo, J. T., & Berntson, G. G. (1992). Social psychological contributions to the decade of the brain: Doctrine of multilevel analysis. *American Psychologist, 47,* 1019–1028.

5. Wadman, R., Durkin, K., & Conti-Ramsden, G. (2011). Social stress in young people with specific language impairments. *Journal of Adolescence, 34*(3), 421–431.

6. Steele, C. M., & Aronson, J. (1995). Stereotype threat and the intellectual test performance of African-Americans. *Journal of Personality and Social Psychology,* 69, 797–811.

7. "Redlining" was coined by John McKnight in the 1960s.

8. "Credit rationing" is the limiting of credit to borrowers who demand funds, even if the borrowers are willing to pay higher interest rates.

9. Also see John Ogbu's work on voluntary and involuntary minorities. Obbu, J. (1998). Voluntary and involuntary minorities: A cultural-ecological theory of school performance with some implications for education. *Anthropology & Education, 29*(2), 155–188.

CHAPTER 3

1. Foster, M. (1997). *Black teachers on teaching.* New York: The New Press.

2. Ladson-Billings, Gloria. (1994). *The dreamkeepers: Successful teachers of African American children.* New York: Jossey-Bass.

3. Reed-Danahay, D. (2000). Habitus and cultural identity: Home/school relationships in rural France. In B. A. U. Levinson et al. (Eds.), *Schooling the symbolic animal: Social and cultural dimensions of education* (pp. 223–236). Lanham, MD: Rowman & Littlefield Publishers.

4. Hanushek, E. A., Kain, J. F., & Rivkin, S. G. (2002). Inferring program effects for specialized populations: Does special education raise achievement for students with disabilities? *Review of Economics and Statistics, 84*(4), 584–599.

5. Anderson, Melinda. (2016, September 28). Even Black preschool teachers are biased. *The Atlantic.* Retrieved from: https://www.theatlantic.com/education/archive/2016/09/the-high-standard-set-by-black-teachers-for-black-students/501989/.

6. Easton-Brooks, D. (2013). Ethnic-matching in urban education. In H. R. Milner & L. Kofu (Eds.), *The handbook on urban education* (pp. 97–113). New York: Taylor & Francis.

7. Egalite, A. J., Kisida, B., & Winters, M. J. (2015). Representation in the classroom: The effect of own-race/ethnicity teacher assignment on student achievement. *Economics of Education Review, 45*, 44–52.

8. Woodson, Carter Godwin. (1990). *The mis-education of the Negro.* Trenton, NJ: Africa World Press.

9. Anderson, Melinda. (2016, June 21). Where are all the principals of color? *The Atlantic.* Retrieved from: https://www.theatlantic.com/education/archive/2016/06/principals-of-color/488006/.

10. Hanushek, Eric A. (1992). The trade-off between child quantity and quality. *Journal of Political Economy, 100*(1), 84–117.

11. Murnane, Richard. (1975). *The impact of school resources on the learning of inner city children.* Cambridge, MA: Ballinger Publishing.

12. Clewell, Beatriz C., Puma, Michael J., & McKay, Shannon A. (2005, April). *Does it matter if my teacher looks like me? The impact of teacher race and ethnicity on student academic achievement.* Paper presented at the Annual Meeting of the American Educational Research Association, Montreal, Canada.

13. Lewis, C. W. (2006). African American male teachers in public schools: An examination of three urban school districts. *Teachers College Record, 108*(2), 224–245.

14. Milner, H. R. (2006). The promise of Black teachers' success with Black students. *Educational Foundations, 20*(3–4), 89–104.

15. Eddy, C. M., & Easton-Brooks, D. (2011). Ethnic matching, school placement, and mathematics achievement of African American students from kindergarten through fifth grade. *Urban Education, 46*(6), 1280–1299.

16. Easton-Brooks, D., & Davis, A. (2007). Wealth, traditional SES indicators, and the achievement debt. *Journal of Negro Education, 76*(4), 530–541.

17. Ainsworth-Darnell, James W. (2002). Why does it take a village? The mediation of neighborhood effects on educational achievement. *Social Forces, 81*, 117–152.

18. Rimm-Kaufman, S. E., & Pianta, R. C. (2000). An ecological perspective on the transition to kindergarten: A theoretical framework to guide empirical research. *Journal of Applied Developmental Psychology, 21*, 491–511.

19. Dee, Thomas. (2004). Teachers, race, and student achievement in a randomized experiment. *Review of Economics and Statistics, 86*(1), 195–210.

20. Easton-Brooks, D. (2015). Bridging the gap: Teacher education. In L. Drakeford (Ed.), *The race controversy in American education.* (p. 259–281). Santa Barbara, CA: Praeger Publishing.

21. Ferguson, R. F. (1998). Teachers' perceptions and expectations and the African American-White test score gap. In C. Jencks & M. Phillips (Eds.), *The Black-White test score gap* (pp. 273–317). Washington, DC: Brookings Institution Press.

22. King, John, & Darling-Hammond, Linda. (2018, May 18). OPINION: We're not doing enough to support teachers of color. *The Hechinger Report.* Retrieved from: https://hechingerreport.org/opinion-we-arent-doing-enough-to-support-teachers-of-color/.

23. Lynn, Marvin. (2006). Education for the community: Exploring the culturally relevant practice of Black male teachers. *Teachers College Record, 108*(12), 2497–2522.

CHAPTER 4

1. Gay, G. (2010). *Culturally responsive teaching: Theory, practice, & research.* New York: Teacher College.

2. See Sonia Nieto's book *Affirming Diverse.*

3. Dr. Patricia Hills-Collins describes "intercept" or "intersectionality" as opening up the possibility of seeing and understanding that multiple spaces of cross-cutting cultural interests can meet. This approach compels us to see, and look for, other spaces where cultural systems come together. Competing intercepts suggest that strong, opposing cultural frameworks may make it challenging to connect cross-cultural frameworks.

4. See Barolome, L. (1994). Beyond the methods fetish: Toward a humanizing pedagogy. *Harvard Educational Review, 64*(2), 173–195.

5. See Kneebone, Elizabeth, & Berube, Alan. (2013). *Confronting suburban poverty in America.* (p. 19). Washington, DC: Brookings Institution Press.

6. Matisa, C. E. (2017). *Feeling white: Whiteness, emotionality, and education.* Boston, MA: Sense Publishers.

7. Duckworth, A. L., Peterson, C., Matthews, M. D., & Kelly, D. R. (2007). Grit: Perseverance and passion for long-term goals. *Journal of Personality and Social Psychology, 9*, 1087–1101.

8. Lynn, M. (2002). Critical race theory and the perspectives of Black men teachers in the Los Angeles schools. *Equity and Excellence in Education, 35*, 119–130.

9. See Louis R. Harlan. (Ed.). (1974). *The Booker T. Washington Papers* (Vol. 3). (pp. 583–587). Urbana, IL: University of Illinois Press.

CHAPTER 5

1. The phrase "social pedagogy" was coined by Jean-Jacques Rousseau. Kornbeck, J., & Rosendal Jensen, N. (2009). *The diversity of social pedagogy in Europe.* Bremen: Europäischer Hochschulverlag.
2. See Kornbeck, J., & Jensen, N. (2009). *The diversity of social pedagogy in Europe.* Bremen: Europäischer Hochschulverlag.
3. Freire, P. (2006). *Pedagogy of the oppressed, 30th anniversary ed.* New York: Continuum.

CHAPTER 6

1. Johnson, J., Showalter, D., Klein, R., & Lester, C. (2014). *Why rural matters 2013–2014: The condition of rural education in the 50 states.* Washington, DC: Rural School and Community Trust.
2. Easton-Brooks, D. (2013). Ethnic-matching in urban education. In H. R. Milner & L. Kofu (Eds.), *The handbook on urban education* (pp. 97–113). New York: Taylor & Francis.
3. The Schools and Staffing Survey (SASS) was conducted by the National Center of Education Statistics (NCES) between 1987 through 2011. SASS was an integrated study on public and private school districts, schools, principals, and teachers designed to provide descriptive data on the context of elementary and secondary education. SASS covered a wide range of topics from teacher demand, teacher and principal characteristics, general conditions in schools, principals' and teachers' perceptions of school climate and problems in their schools, teacher compensation, district hiring, and retention practices, to basic characteristics of the student population.
4. National Education Association (2018, September 26). "NEA and teacher recruitment: An overview." Retrieved from: http://nea.org/home/29031.htm.
5. Boser, U. (2011). *Teacher diversity matters: A state-by-state analysis of teachers of color.* Center for American Progress.
6. Sleeter, C. (2017). Critical race theory and the whiteness of teacher education. *Urban Education, 15*(2), 155–169.
7. Easton-Brooks, D., Robinson, D., & Williams, S. M. (2018). Schools in transition: Creating a diverse school community. In R. Goings & J. Young (Eds.), *Teachers College Record 2018 Yearbook: The Every Student Succeeds Act: Critical multicultural perspectives from the field.* (pp. 1–26). Teachers College Record.

CHAPTER 7

1. Pathways2Teaching is a concurrent enrollment program designed for eleventh- and twelfth-grade students to explore teaching as potential career choice while examining critical issues related to educational justice and earning college credit. Since

2010, the Pathways2Teaching program has served hundreds of students in several Denver metro school districts and through its affiliate program in eastern Oregon. Many of its graduates are now enrolled in teacher education programs or in other related areas, such as social work.

2. Bianco, M., Leech, N., & Mitchell, K. (2011). Pathways to teaching: African American male teens explore teaching as a career. *The Journal of Negro Education, 80*(3), 368–383.

3. Villagomez, A., Easton-Brooks, D., Lubbes, T., & Gomez, K. (2016). Oregon Teacher Pathway: Responding to national trend. *Equity & Excellence in Education, 49*(1), 100–114.

4. Call Me Mister: The program combines the special strengths and resources of Clemson University with individualized instructional programs offered by several colleges and universities in South Carolina. To provide even greater opportunity and access, students have the option of first attending a two-year partner college before transferring to a four-year institution to complete their baccalaureate degree. In addition, the project has limited enrollment in an MA in teaching program.

5. See Gist, C. D., White, T., & Bianco, M. (2018). "Pushed" to teach: Pedagogies and policies for a Black women educator pipeline. *Education and Urban Society, 50*(1), 56–86.

6. See Institute for Teachers of Color Committed to Racial Justice (ITOC). Led by Dr. Rita Kohi, it provides an annual three-day professional development event to facilitate the growth, success, and retention of teachers of color who work in public schools serving students of color, with ongoing structures of networking and continued site-based support. A unique collaboration between the disciplines of teacher education, educational leadership, and ethnic studies, this national conference rigorously selects approximately one hundred ITOC fellows each summer to cultivate their racial justice leadership capacities as educational change agents.

7. For H.E.L.L.A., see author Farima Pour-Khorshild's work: H.E.L.L.A.: Collective *testimonio* that speak to the healing, empowerment, love, liberation, and action embodied by social justice educators of color. In the *Association of Mexican American Educators Journal, 10*(2), 16–32.

8. Project IMPACT: Increasing Male Practitioners and Classroom Teachers. Its mission is to increase the representation of males from racially and ethnically diverse backgrounds in teaching and respond to persistent opportunity gaps faced by young men from diverse backgrounds. Many of the student participants will come from underserved environments and will want to utilize education to contribute to the socioeconomic and educational transformation of these communities. IMPACT focuses on incoming freshmen at Rowan University and provides resources and supports as they continue through their college career. IMPACT participants are high-achieving students who have demonstrated a commitment to academic excellence and community engagement.

Index

First Natives. *See* Native American
Florida Fund for Minority Teachers, 24
Foster, Michele, ix, 113
Freire, Paulo, 69

Gay, Geneva L., ix–xiv, 70, 94–95,
    95–96, 103, 106–107, 113
gender, 3, 31–32, 87;
    female, 17;
    male, 14, 16, 108
grit, 60–61

Hawaii, 2, 93
heritage, ix, x, 26, 27
Healing, Empowerment, Love,
    Liberation, and Action (H.E.L.L.A.),
    112
Hills-Collins, Patricia, 79
Hispanic-serving institutions (HSI), 100,
    111
Historically Black Colleges and
    Universities (HBCU), 23–24, 88,
    100, 111, 112
Hmong, 5
home culture, 6, 25–26, 27, 40–41,
    43–44, 57
Houston, xvii, 84;
    Houston Independent School District
    (HISD), 4
Houston,Charles H., 30

immigrants, xii–xiii, 5–6, 13, 20, 21–22,
    26, 50, 62, 71, 72, 86, 91
immigration, 50, 72, 76
Increasing Male Practitioners and
    Classroom Teachers (IMPACT), 104,
    112
inferiority, 34, 79
injustice, 47, 61–40, 62, 64, 69, 75
inner-city, 45, 47, 84

Institute for Teachers of Color
    Committed to Racial Justice (ITOC),
    112
Institute for Urban Education, 96
Intentional actions, 34, 68–69, 69–70,
    72, 77, 94, 103, 105–106, 107, 112,
    115, 117
Intentionality, 68–77, 103, 105, 114,
    115, 117
Iowa, 4, 93
irresponsible teachers, 71–74

Japanese, 5;
    Japanglish, 21
Justice, advocate for, 41, 61–64, 76, 91

Kansas City, 45, 96
Konglish, 21
Kohi, Rita, 114

Ladson-Billings, Gloria, xii, 103, 106–
    107, 113, 114
Lynn, Marvin, 114

Maine, 4, 91–92, 93
maginalization, 28, 29–30, 102–103,
    105–106
mathematics, 4–7, 17, 30, 32–33, 58,
    62–63, 64, 114–115
mental stress, 12, 13, 57, 71, 77, 110,
    113–114
mental triggers, 17–18
Mexican, 50, 54, 76, 104
Miami-Dade County Public Schools, 4
Mien, 5
Milner, Rich, 94–95, 96
Ministry of Education of Palau,
    Micronesia, 38
Minnesota, 4, 5–6
minority(ies), 1–3, 14, 24, 40–41, 93
Montana, 84–85

About the Author

Dr. Donald Easton-Brooks is a leader, researcher, and activist for equity in education. He is best known as a critical cultural quantitative researcher and uses advanced statistical analysis to examine the impact of educational policies and practice on the academic experience and outcomes of students of color. He has been instrumental in introducing ethnic matching to the field of education. His findings on this topic include the fact that the academic scores of students of color are significantly higher in reading and mathematics when these students have at least one teacher of color in their academic career. His work in ethnic matching and teacher quality has been used to influence policies both nationally and internationally. His work has also contributed to creating programs to increase equity in education and for educators of color in several states.